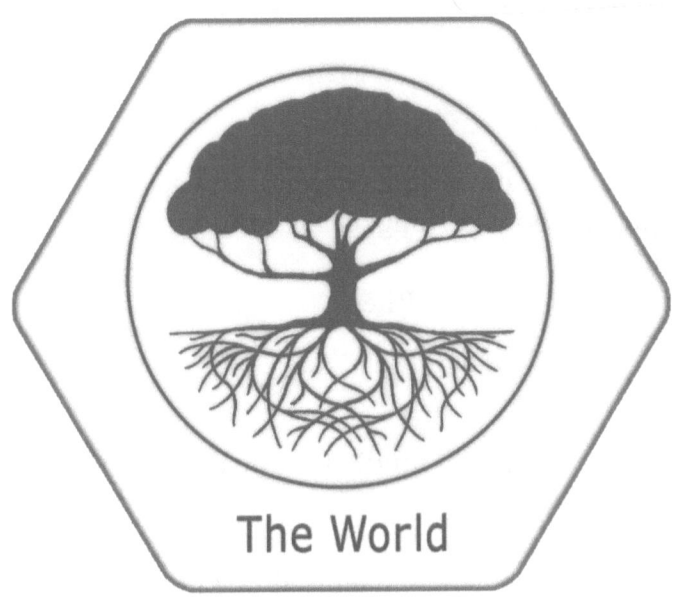

The World

Documents For The Reader

Companion Book For Stone Riley's Tarot Decks

By Stone Riley

To my Goddesses and Gods,
and to you the reader,
in love, respect, thanks and praise
this work is dedicated.

Philosophic Note
The thinking in this book is profoundly
influenced by the Seth Material
and deeply indebted to the work of
Jane Roberts and Robert Butts.

Table Of Contents

Continued
Table Of Contents

List Of Illustrations

Continued
List Of Illustrations

Foreword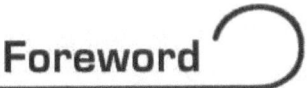

By Deborah Jarvis

A real kind of writer does exist, one who transcends the word slavery of the student and the easy slide of writing for pleasure. One who is in the passionate embrace of their muse, in it fully, one for whom that lovemaking calls forth an issue that is joy for the writer and the reader too. This writer seldom spells their meaning out, instead allowing the reader space to contemplate meanings.

For a collection of works like this it's hard to write an introduction, hard to capture such an immortal mind on a page of mortal words. I thought it would be simple when Stone approached me for an introduction to this volume. I thought: This should be simple, seeing that I've known him for years. I've read his works, had him read my future and fortune multiple times. It should be easy. Then after reading the book I took up writing several times but could not get a grasp on how to do it.

Like for a beginning student burdened by words, the words had to be dragged onto the page and sense had to be beaten into them. They would not flow. I thought, I'm a writer. What's wrong with me? I finally gave up for a long while. But then finally my muse woke me with a kick on a cool Saturday morning at five a.m. At long last I could write.

All writers depend on their muses to some extent. For some the muse is omnipresent. Stone has been on excellent terms with his muse for a long time, and it shows. Stone's visual art is lovely but abstract – I am no lover of abstract art – yet his pictures speak to me in the same way his poetry does. Neither form speaks directly, both certainly are often unclear, but meaning does come clear if you look and look again.

There are no simple verses in this thin volume, not in the visual art or poems or stories. Of course Stone's tale of meeting the love of his life comes to mind. Perhaps this is a simple theme, and familiar, but here is actually a celebration of the union of souls long destined for each other. This becomes, in fact, the kind of love we all dream to have but never dare to speak beyond a whisper, for fear some god with beetled brow will show disfavor and deny us.

So open this book as the transcendent item that it is, dear reader. Walk through its pages then return here that much wiser, that much richer and, in all ways, more wholly and more truly you. You will not regret the trip. Along the way you will have witnessed at least some portion of what the muses can teach us in this modern age of reason and machines. You will have seen proof that underneath it all, and through it all, a sense of wonder is still moving.

How I Started In Tarot And You Can Too

Document #1

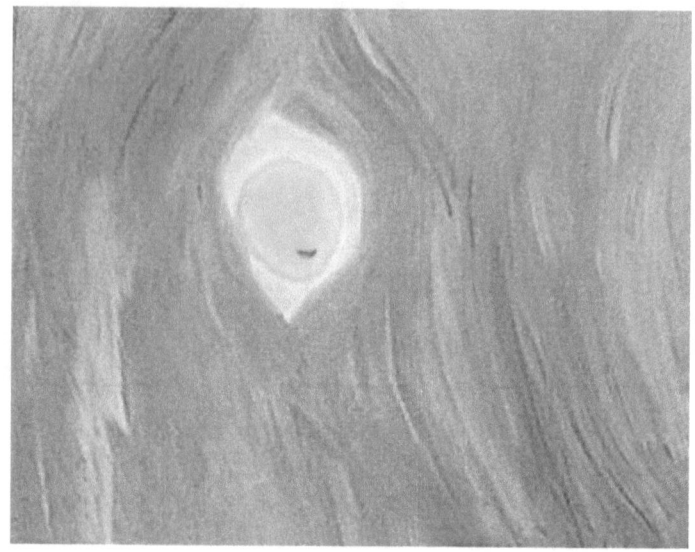

"A Friend Visits The Studio"
Painting on canvas by SR

> How To Start Reading Tarot

Note: Your experience having serious conversations with people about life's difficulties will be far more useful than any prior Tarot experience. Also: If you're thinking of doing readings for yourself, while you study these suggestions pretend you are both the people mentioned.

If you have an easy reading deck – like Simple Tarot, Spirit Hill, or many others – here's a good method to try first.

Sit at a table with your client (or with yourself). Turn all the cards face up and glance at them quite informally. Pick a few to show, saying each card makes a statement about life and altogether they can tell every story. Say many people over many years developed Tarot as a tool to help us sort out our confusions.

Now ask the client for help doing this: Turn the cards face down and mix them all around. Then, with the cards still facing down, spread them neatly across to left and right.

Ask the client to choose an important aspect of their life situation and bring it into mind, something where they'd like good advice, or a hint of how to see things truthfully and usefully. Say it does not need to be huge, but must be some issue in their life for which they honestly could use a bit of good advice or a wise impartial explanation. You can trust that all discussion which is needed will arise from this.

Suggest that if they want to close their eyes they can and say that when their issue is extremely vivid in their mind, as real and vivid as can be, please reach out and pick a card. When they do so, have them turn the card face up and look. Ask them what it says, in both its picture and its words. Ask if this maybe says something about their issue.

Looking at the card's words and picture yourself, give keen attention to everything the client says. If you need elaboration to take their meaning, courteously ask. If a bit of wisdom comes to mind you feel you ought to say, politely and kindly offer that.

But what inner voices should you give attention when you dare offering a client wisdom? I'm sure at that moment you'd rather not be listening to your prejudices, envies, peevish discontents and petty bickerings, your self-indulgent self-deceits and crippling fears, etc. You want a voice something like your natural, healthy, sane, creative, joyful, free and loving self.

If you are not yet accustomed to the amazing powers of intuition we all have, common property of our human race, first listen to whatever lessons you have learned in life yourself, and maybe to some philosophy of life you like, maybe some school of thought from some wise teacher you admire. But definitely find a voice of love and optimism in those sources.

You will find other sources going forward. With effort you'll learn fast in this work, gaining excellent truths from clients, from the philosophy that's written in the Tarot deck, and from startling revelations about your own life that will appear. You will find the sort of courage that's needed.

So your effort is rewarded: You begin to recognize the voice of reliable intuition. You may come to recognize it by its color, so to speak, or by its musical tone perhaps, or by the direction from which it enters your mental space, etc. I expect you'll recognize it by its insistence that you give full attention, and the exact precision of things it says when you do.

Of course when I call this a voice, you know it can be non-voice sounds, pictures you are shown, scents, floods of emotion, a memory of your life as an example of what's meant, etc., but on opening your full attention while examining the card's words and picture, you discover a specific meaning you may tell. The card gives a vital a hint.

But you'll also find that many errors teach moderation in your growing confidence: A toothache may distract you. Or you might have two clients there together and say things to one that should be given to the other. Of course telling a prediction can stop it from coming true. It seems the past can be altered too. There might come some startling spirit from the dead. You'll later think of things you should have said. So forth.

But in reading Tarot one hazard is above all else: As with any voice, what you perceive in the voice of intuition will be limited or opened by your beliefs and expectations. And this sad situation equally: You will very often find the client cannot hear what you are saying because there is some fascinating fear or shame that holds their attention riveted instead.

But when your path brings you to this work you'll do it. You will simply do the best you can, with a firm and patient kindly manner resting in the faith this work is good.

Or you might take my word on this: We strive to bring things into consciousness because human consciousness is the decisive governor of human life. Amid the universal dance of infinite creativity, each person's allotment of the universal mind, in subtle complex ways, through its conscious choices makes their body and their fate.

So we use Tarot – like other suchlike implements since human life and mind began – to lead our consciousness in keenly sharp attention step by step bravely into our thoughts so thus our choices can be re-made wiser. Thus reality, in its divine pleasure, sees and loves itself. You, doing this, are thus a priestly guide of souls through an enchanted wood, like, in my youth, I once saw painted on an ancient cup from Greece.

Proceed as needed with more cards, on the same or other issues. Feel free to point out details of an issue to the client, or request clarification from them, even courteously interrupting if you must. Feel free to ask for clarification from the cards as well, then pull a card or two and tell the client what they say. Feel free to pray, but silently.

When otherwise finished, I like to finally ask the deck this question: "Please tell us what else we should know." If you take this practice, pull and read a card or two.

When all seems finished, I customarily express, aloud or silently, gratitude to whatever mind or spirit of this here deck that I imagine, and so I close the deck respectfully.

I finally hold the client's hands, if they allow, and quite sincerely say, "Thank you for your trust," under-standing that they teach me, knowing that their trust is holy.

> Further Study

There are many books, good and bad, about Tarot. Some books might probably be useful to you, but the best teacher is undoubtedly the deck itself.

I suggest this study: Get a Tarot deck with pictures that seem to speak to you, even if they are speaking vaguely. Now, on the first morning of a week choose some cards, 3 or 4 or more or less, and put them in your pocket. That week, watch for those cards in the world around.

Maybe make a poem and a picture when a card appears. That's how my first deck was created. Or you might discuss the work with friends, which was delightful, or eat and sing and dance, consume intoxicating substances, or keep a diary.

Continue till the world shows every card or till you quit.

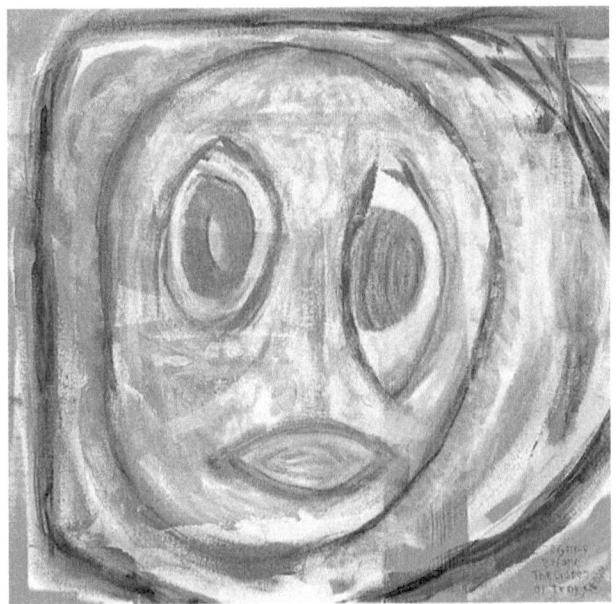

"Odysseus Before The Gates Of Troy"
Painting on canvas by SR
(a self-portrait in confusion)

> How I Started In Tarot,
My Hope, Purpose & Procedure

I first made the Simple Tarot, my first deck in its
first edition, as a way to start my self-taught art career
and step decisively into real human life. That is to say,
to find the values that I wished to live for and a strategy
by which to live.

The project occupied my concentrated effort for one
year, early January 1980 to early January 1981. At that time
I was emerging from the unremitting concentrated stress
of youthful death defying politics around the Vietnam War
and arriving in the working poverty of a young family man.
By some coincidence, January 1980 was the 10th anniversary
of my month in military jail for war resistance work.

The goal I had in mind was to set down what I had
learned about life so far in a form that would be a clear start-

ing point for whatever lay ahead, and to learn from that study. I did not want to lose my dead and living and all of the beautiful and dreadful failures and successes, for I was aware that all those things so alive for me then, those things of my true reality, could fade into forgetfulness. Tarot seemed to offer help with this.

By then, by early 1980, I had been reading Tarot for my education in private moments for a while. I was using the Rider Waite and the Aquarian Tarots. The Rider was a fundamental sketch of modern culture, done by a theatrical designer with india ink and flat watercolor 70 years before, whereas the Aquarian was recent, in poster inks in the somber colors and flower shapes that were current reality in my eyes then. So I would read the two decks together for a fuller view of life. As you might expect, that also gave a better view of Tarot reading itself.

For my purposes I felt Tarot's claim to universal human truth held a tantalizing savor. Could I really, as purported by its theorists and more or less confirmed by my limited experience, use the Tarot deck structure as a diagram on which to scribble everything I knew of human life?

And if I could do that, if its structure really could be trusted that far, wouldn't Tarot also definitely help me reach conclusions, fill in the many blanks of my experience, and thus remember much that I would otherwise never even understand? Wouldn't that help a lot in going forward to a worthy life?

I was programming computers by then (my good brother, an engineer, had advised I might do well in that profession) and, surprisingly, insight came to the project through thinking like a coder. In that mode I recognized Tarot as a recording and playback system for human life wisdom. Then, in examining this device, coder thinking quickly offered a convincing list of main design objectives. There were 3.

Objective 1: I should try to make an actual Tarot deck that was actually useful to me. Scribbling my experiences on a set of blank cards, so to speak, following the deck's authentic outline, ought to do that. The deck is supposedly a whole diagram of life so its structure could be a list of questions to ask my memories, checked against real life around me now. I must be very truthful but the versions of the cards on hand would help as prompts.

Objective 2: If I truly learned about life by creating a Tarot deck from my life, it would be useful for other people also. I'd be adding recent local accent and color, but it would be useful for others because, in learning, I would use Tarot's "coding sheet" to map my life onto human nature. The Tarot structure supposedly has recorded data about our common human life far beyond an individual's share of data. The data is all merged when a reading is done, and merged with the reader's data too.

Objective 3: On studying the matter, I came to think the time was good to do this work. Our culture world was doing major change but there was an ancient simple style of poetry and picture – the style of Zen and Tao and the like which I was already studying – that spoke very clearly to us there on the New Age leading edge.

So I thought cards in that artistic style might be strong clear prompts to imagination for many people, serving as the Rider Waite has in its time, but in our cultural moment and going forward, a version of the deck to be a wise enduring guide for many future people.

Therefore, besides the personal attractions of the project, and its urgent nature to me personally, it seemed perhaps to also be a way of doing useful politics.

You see, Tarot works very well. Tarot, and many other systems like it all across the world through history, reliably give people information that they do not have, often breaking chains of misunderstanding their society has loaded on them.

And it's easy. First you find a divination tool that speaks your language so you understand, some version of Tarot perhaps. Then you go into the proper willful, attentive and receptive frame of mind and ask a question. Then you pick a Tarot card and turn it up (or some such gesture) and give attention. A bit of new accurate information or a good answer or an apt suggestion appears in your mind as if in human conversation with some wise person.

(How does it work? Either by some excellent illusion in our human mental processes or else through some surprising fact about time and space and all of that, or both. I have further guesses but here I'll just say that.)

And you also see, the times were different then than now. Then it seemed that truth itself in any quantity was likely to be revolutionary for the good. The madness then was lies.

In our time now, early December 35 years later, another new report of disgusting despicable crass cruel brutality by our government, all for the insane greed of the ruling class, was just released, one more of many such, and nothing will be done. In these times great heaps of truth pile up and our good revolution consists of any action toward fulfilling truth's demands.

Back then, when I was first considering a project in Tarot, truth itself was missing. I was trying to assess my project's possible value to the world, thinking of it as a lifetime work perhaps, feeling optimistic that it might be widely used, and we were in a time of lies, lies on a very wide and yet pervasively intimate scale, as though lies were the air you breathed. Any fresh breath of truth might help reveal the poison stink.

I'll tell you one particular example of those times. This bit of it infuriated me: I knew my fellow citizens were mostly still in love with our U.S. national propaganda lies.

There was a nonsense question you could ask: "Do you think America is the greatest country in the world?"

This was nonsense on its face of course. To give a rational reply, a person must assign some kind of "greatness" score to every country in the world, do a sort, then observe America's location in the resulting scale.

But all the Americans I asked, with rare exception, would actually do precisely this: Listen to my question, think for a moment and see the difficulties of the question, decide to abandon thought, often shrug, and answer "Yes, I think America is the greatest country in the world."

They were doing this even after the horrors of the very horrid Vietnam War that were just recently gone by, vast horrors done by our soldiers from the very start of it and repeated constantly with increasing pitch of desperation right to the end, horrors mostly done by public order of our generals in fulfillment of our government's public policies and constantly reported clearly in the daily news; yes it was even then after those long recent years of vast and quite intentional evil, that enormous spasm of pointless insane furious destruction, it was then in 1980 and I was finding most Americans still clung somehow to their cherished lie that our country, unlike most other countries, is noble and does good.

But of course that was only one example of those dire and dark unlighted times. It was a very clear demonstrable example but certainly not the worst thing by far.

For as well it was quite evident by then that the world is dying soon, by atomic war and/or by global warming, unless we drastically revolutionized the way our country was run, unless we instituted real democracy to some significant degree, as many of us cogently proposed. But of course no hope was visible for that in 1980, after we had seen the ruling class power straight through the Civil Rights Movement, tossing corpses left and right, riding their huge undaunted economic system of racist classiest burn and pillage robbery.

You'll understand that this was personal with me. They had made an enemy of me and in that struggle I had found my being.

I had come up as a working class poor so-called "White" boy in an ugly industrial dangerous city of the racist Jim Crow South and also thus as a perfect target of the U.S. Army draft. If by chance I missed the empire's foreign wars then I was meant to spend a life at labor in quite poisonous industrial facilities where constant injury and death were merely "accidents".

But I was independent thinking and smart, always reading news and classics, at least smart and free enough – like more and more of the so-called "White" youth of the South – to see with opening eyes the world which had been built for us.

And this seemed starkly plain to me: I was unavoidably in war against my government, their American Permanent Race War, their Vietnam War, their Big Business Class War (a.k.a. the War Against The Earth), their Atomic Bomb Insane Cold War, all being the same thing and me being fodder for the machine one way or another.

Further, I shall here pass by almost unsaid the murder of a friend in war, and other tragedies observed in that long time, injustices which seemed to be enough true confirmation of my inclination to the struggle. For in several cases my reactions and actions did seem to confirm that I could do some thing, some small thing, of proper use and value in the tests.

So when it did happen, immediately when it was made – when the first copy of the first edition of the Simple Tarot cards came off my art work table into a pocket size box – and then when immediately this product of my eye and hand and heart found good uses in the genuine little personal paths of the constant struggle for democracy – then it did seem the strategy by which to live my further life, and the values toward which I wished to spend that life, had come clear.

Now, with all the several hundred little bits of good that I have used that deck to do in 35 years, the counseling and the teaching – and maybe 40 handmade copies I have given out as free and whatever good they may have done – for this does seem to be a baseline version of Tarot in our culture, deep and usable by everyone – yet now, on writing this account of the beginning, my big ambition that Simple Tarot would be famous does seem ironic, even embarrassing to my pride, as though I am too wise for silly pride, or to be so wise I must pretend.

Whereas in fact, that ambition at the start now seems too small. Certainly my project needs enlargement – it must be richer and deeper than one deck in one artistic style – but 35 years practicing a variety of arts enlarged my muscularity enough for that. And also our world has changed profoundly, democracy at last publicly awakened, which I think makes it more likely to be helped by Tarot.

Looking back now from this new beginning, the ambition for my first deck's fame did get my effort started, bringing enough real achievements that I could accept the years of challenge as an aspiring Master Student of Tarot.

That first deck made a healing teaching priest of me. It also was a rich and supple root stock for further art work, most of all so far the Spirit Hill Tarot doubling the project now. I even seem to see the whole thing's outline, with its 3rd Tarot to be in artistically new dimensions, tracing a Pythagorean diagram of some prismatic lens.

So yes, my project has lived and grown. It might grow to be a sturdy straw in the brick walls humanity is building. Or is that straining metaphor a fantasy again? Really, can

Tarot help our world survive? Or will the human world survive at all?

Our human world – this place we all by our conscious-ness collectively create – has changed profoundly in my time here. We still have blind greed and fear in plenty – enough to kill us all perhaps – but, speaking of a total balance, I've seen our world's beliefs grow to be far more deeply and richly realistic.

When I was young, entering adult awareness 50 years ago, it was bewildering to see thinkers of every occupation and philosophy exert themselves deciding which precepts of White Supremacy they would accept and which deny. This one amused me: A prominent historian proposed that civilized citizens of any race are mentally advanced beyond uncivilized barbarians of any race and, coincidentally, there are no White uncivilized barbarians. That theory was con-sidered erudite and liberal.

A momentous half century later now, excited news reports give frequent coverage of competing theories about the origin of the human race. These theories differ – by pointing to many different facts we know – but they all pro-pose that all humans have had the same mental equipment for about the last 250,000 years, through all of known history and prehistory too, utterly regardless of "civilization" and of skin color.

As well, historians now thrill to lurid revelations of White Supremacy, trying to understand, with thorough scholarship and gripping real life drama, how all that cruelty happened, mourning that it did and lionizing the resisters.

And the current rising of our democracy against it is very beautiful. January 2015: Across our country White Supremacist so-called "peace officers" murder hundreds of unarmed citizens per year in a terror campaign supporting their vast neo-slavery prison industry. After an especially

disgusting murder, local citizens rose in mass under excellent voluntary discipline, immediately developed a clear bold
careful tactical vision that found nationwide public mass
support, and they are still up in action months later.

I mean to say, White Supremacy has been excreted
from our culture's thinking, although it still can be found
lying about in big piles of odorous non-thinking that we
step into too much.

I mean to say, ceasing to believe White Supremacy
brought tremendous mental liberation in America overall.
Just like very many of our non- so-called "White" poets
and philosophers had constantly predicted for very many
years, when we adjudged our Permanent Race War, our most
pervasive longest war, a crime – when we, in our democracy,
declared the biggest propaganda lie a lie – then our democracy awoke in many ways.

And I claim that great case as an example for my lesser
case: I say that piece of history supports my proposal that
Tarot will help our world survive.

And from personal experience I say: Tarot speaks
inside your truest self saying that you are a being with
the rest, thus declaring The War Against The Earth to be
a crime. Tarot helps fill an aching need for proof of our
universal companionship, thus it helps establish certainty
that human ownership of Earth is only fragile lies.

I say – similar to the history I cite above plus from my
own experience – Tarot helps to reassure our love for
truth that love for truth can realistically arise in bold
actions.

I'm hearing currently from persons such as Klein,
Brand, Tippett, Berry, Solnit, Hedges, Roberts, West, Starhawk
and McKibbon – echoing the voices in my youth of Ella
Baker and Dr. King – that a new mysticism is needed in our
politics now. (From some I'm paraphrasing this, others

quoting.) It seems a new mysticism is the missing piece of our good revolution.

Example: If a human "owns" a mountain and a valley, our current "law" is such the person may explode the mountain into dust and truck the dust into the valley. This murderous insanity is called "legal" pursuant to Materialist Individualism, an insane and murderous mysticism of radical loneliness (and raison d'être of The War Against The Earth) that our rulers, in their murderous insanity, proclaim among us as official doctrine.

Our democracy does not possess a counteracting mysticism. Me advising here as a professional magician: We must create a well formed realistic magical belief giving us realistic confidence that we can say "crime against the Earth is murder" and then reliably make it stick, powerfully conjuring from ourselves potently decisive truth enforcing force. (Please see below "Proposals For Our Mystic Doctrine".)

And it seems obvious to me that some commonplace pocket size truth revealing implement would be handy at many moments in that alchemical transformation of our selves.

And later, in the New Age we and our children and their children's children's children thus create – beyond the fiery veil of indecision that we see before us now – then the democratic common use of things like Tarot, etc., would continue to be helpful, as it always has in every human place.

But this is not to say that all is well out there beyond the dark and fiery Veil Of Indecision in that New Age. All is not well there, not even if our democracy does arise in our self transforming truth enforcing bold decisive power very soon, maybe this year 2015, or in the next or next.

Even if we do arise in conscious mystic power very soon, there will be hard and painful work to do – but full of poignant beauty if it's full of love – for our descendants.

The chaos of this Old Age's end has taken hold of Earth already to a great degree, so they ahead of us must first learn to somehow survive in tumult. Then, when survival of the human race is somehow accomplished, they will begin to mourn, for all Earth's dead undoubtedly.

But if we arise very soon – in time to prove conclusively for them the mighty powers of truth and conscious freedom – then amid their sorrow they will also strive, somehow, to heal Her.

> Proposals For Our Mystic Doctrine

#1: The U.S. Civil Rights Movement heroically succeeded brilliantly at freeing minds, but only made small changes in our government and was quite defeated in changing the economy. So we should know those two tasks are given to us. But we are also given the 3 great lessons of non-violent struggle: 1) Non-violent struggle is the only strategy available to us. 2) It must be daring and disruptive. 3) We persuade others by our own willing sacrifice.

#2: As a reader you will need community. In the midst of action I have seen myself as chaplain to our little army, giving things a chaplain gives: Food and clothing, shelter, the proofs of our humanity shown by fine art, hope when you have no hope, wise counsel conjured by whatever magic is on hand, respect. And in the midst of peace I have told stories. Always I have loved and often known that I was loved. I wish you this.

#3: Do not believe the stories that you hear about your soul. Learn about it by your own experience. I am advising this because my soul surprisingly seems to be made entirely of sympathetic keen attention. (A basic substance of the Universe?) I suspect it may be easy to mistake your soul, for mine arrays itself in rich disguises which I guess it puts on voluntarily for reasons currently beyond my understanding. In short, my soul is a mystery. I simply try to work cooperatively with it.

#4 Don't expect new work to go efficiently at first. This rule may be uncomfortable, especially if beginner's luck took you to wonderful success the first time out. It's likely you haven't got the bits of the work sorted yet onto a rational outline whereas in the first try you assigned wise and agile intuition to be the project leader. Don't despair. Do not despair. Your rational self has excellent abilities and works quite efficiently if given healthy goals and not over-stressed.

#5 Take a healthy walk today. If it is in woods or desert, by a river, brook or sea, with mountains on your skyline or a plain, and if the sky is clear around or pledges rain or threatens storms to toss the trees and waves, or if breezes softly play the contours of your face, take your heart out to it in your hands. Take your questions to it. Take your sorrows to it. Listen to it like its child.

> To Be Continued

May we continue these discussions in further documents of this series? My vote is yes. And in particular I calculate we need some poetry, two batches of it, next and further toward the end.

Poems For The Reader : A Gift For You

Document #2

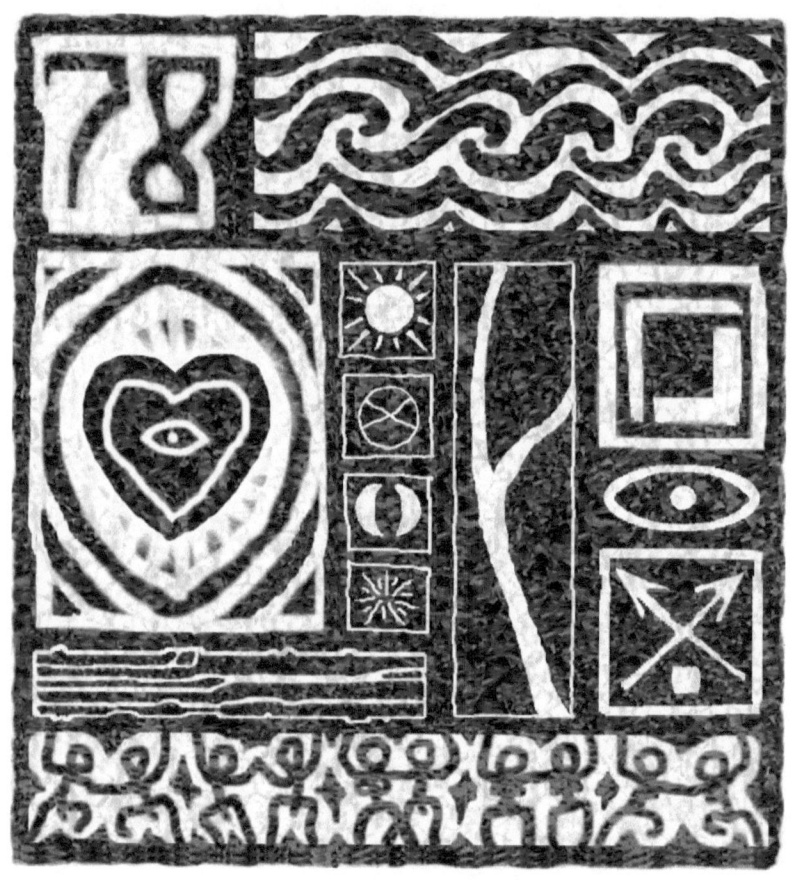

"Tarot Card"
Digital Image by SR

Invitation To A Student Of Tarot

This is a fortune telling system, a magic book,
a diagram of human life and soul
wherein your intuition speaks the truth
your self can never know or soon forgets.

Here is the classic deck of picture cards,
the old city of 78 squares,
the ancient map drawn up as though life were
an ever-shifting game of 78 tiles whereon
each human token at each moment falls.

In this book of pictures, poetry and prose
you will come upon a certain numbering of roads,
a careful survey of the gods and men in their abodes,
a full accounting of the ancestor odes.

Naked, clothe your self in daring
and simply touch the flow of an infinite
and ever-present moment which you know is now;
feel at once the night and morning;
thus come to be like a dolphin touching
echoes in the ever-present sea.

Ask a question, touch a page;
there study what good fortune and your own eye
have to say.
To learn of life just ask for guidance;
your own hand can point the way.

If you wish now, come with me;
stand upon my shoulders as I walk the sea.
Repeat the journey trod when you were young;
hearken to the tale from your own tongue.
At every marker stone embrace the view;

Comprehend the truth and speak it new.

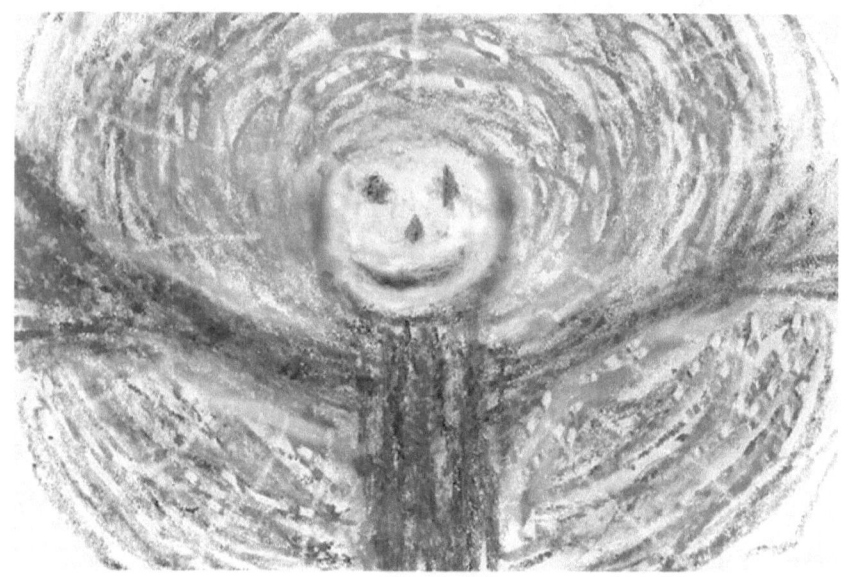

"Beloved Little Child Recovered From Illness"
Drawing with hard crayon on bristol
paper, digitally modified, by SR
(Portrait of my grandchild at six years old.)

0: The Fool

A clown leaps from the height,
this prince, this god of fools.
Unfurling colored wings of immortality
he soars out high. But, drunken
with the dizzy speed and power,
he folds one wing and falls :

                  :

                  :

                  :

to this world.

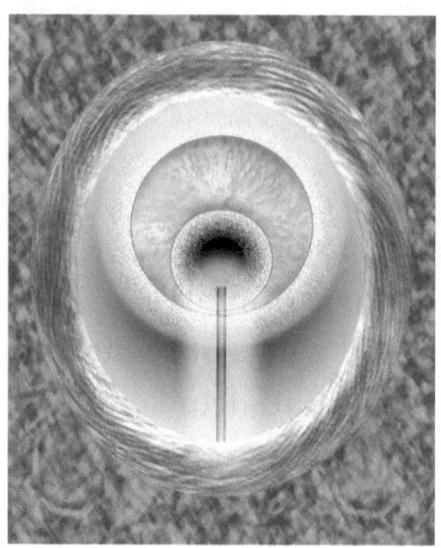

"Image Of One"
Digital image by SR

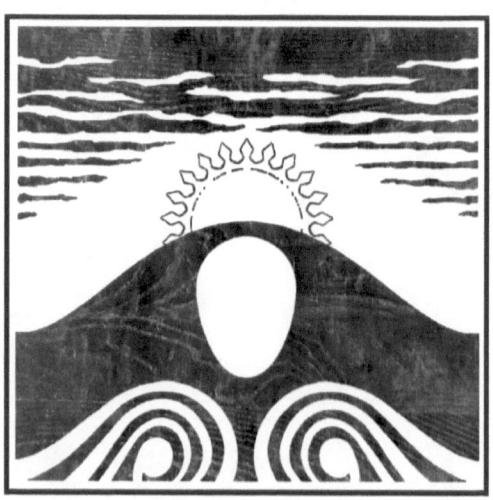

"Image Of Two"
Digital image from a pencil drawing
by SR

1: The Magician

A clot am I
     of earth, wind, fire and water.
A breath am I
     of earth, wind, fire and water.
A spark am I
     of earth, wind, fire and water.
A drop am I
     of earth, wind, fire and water.
And yet I speak !
A human thing
     who names the gods.

2: The High Priestess

Cast your eye to the farthest shore
then cast you heart beyond.
There open your heart
to the velvet touch,
the holy touch of dawn.

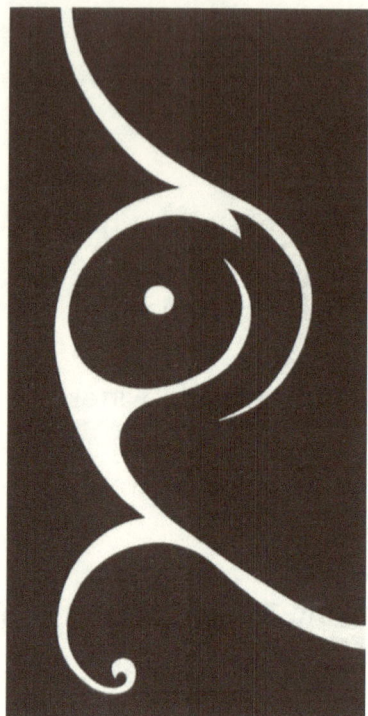

"Egg"
Canvas painting by SR

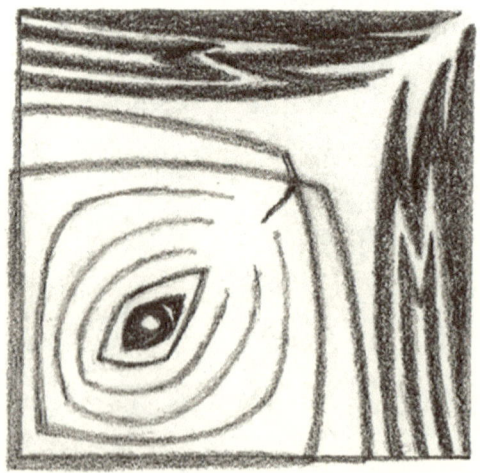

"Breaking Through At Last"
Pencil drawing by SR

3: The Empress

Oh   QUEEN OF HEAVEN
       mistress of our prayers;
Oh   grandmother EVE
       you who first bore child
       and gave it suck,
       you who first laid hand
       upon the newborn human brow;
Oh   PERFECT MOTHER OF US ALL
I,   fruit of your womb,
       call your name BLESSED
       and kneel here at your feet.

4: The Emperor

Oh   honorable father Adam,
       you who measure space
       and count the hours;
Your voice of power
       invigorates both demi-god
       and demon.
You   who cast a legal deed
       upon this shadowy realm
       and stamp a seal
       upon all that is yours;
At will you call the lightening bolt
       or lift a roof beam high.

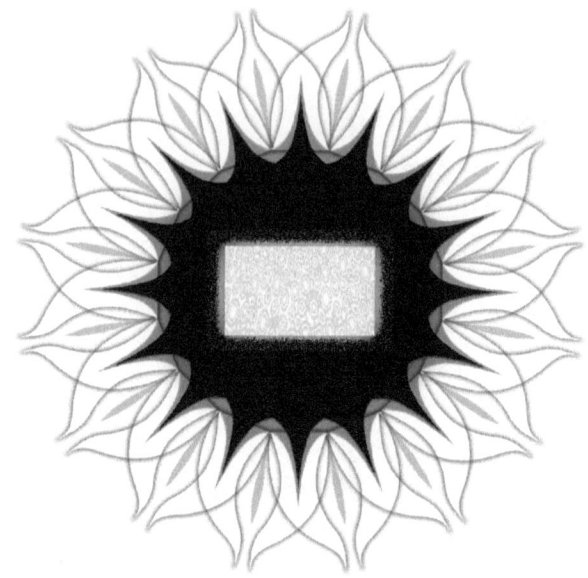

"Preface"
Digital image by SR

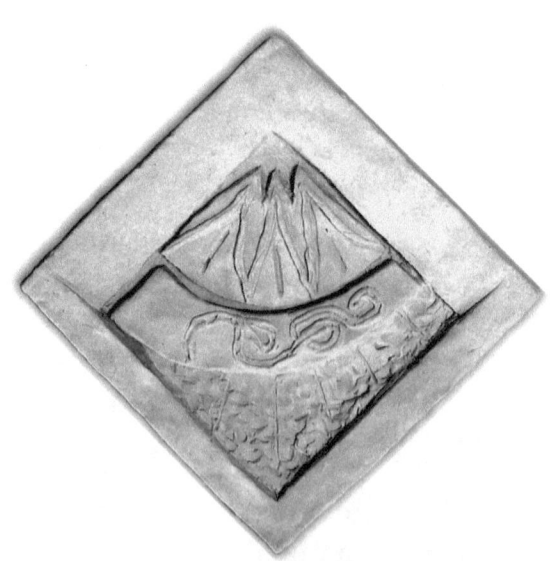

"A Sorcerer's Apprentice"
Polymer clay sculpture by SR

5: The High Priest

This endless eddied world of surge and flow
may here and there forget to know
that it is All
but dreams instead
that it is You
or I.

Yet in each heart will ever lie
the soul's deep pool
the porphyry bowl of lotus wine,
the self-dissolving sigh,
so to my lips
the endless draught you pour.

When I have drunk
and bathed
and drowned
and sunk beneath the waves I've found
my self somehow composed once more
and lifted to a sunlit shore where
wind-soaked flesh
and bony core
become an echoing ocean sound.

So now the eyes within my head look round
surprised to see both You and I
with callused feet on stony ground
still at unbounded ocean's edge
immersed in flowing sky.

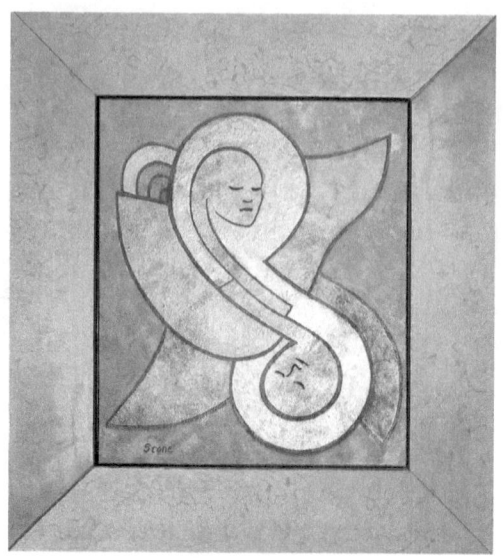

"Together"
Painting on assembled canvas and wood
by SR

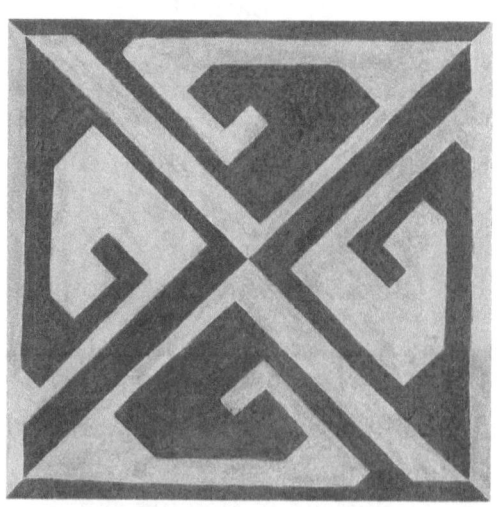

"Alphabeticon Layout Sheet #3"
Painting on loose canvas sheet
by SR

6: The Lovers

Love, thou art perfect in all thy ways,
Perfection whispering on the waters.

(Consider our joys, have they not been
  a strengthening bond these times?
  Do I not know thee fair and well?)

So shed all lies which others tell,
lies of blind hunger, of fearful
jealousy and pitiful defeat.

Gaze into my clear heart
wide, calm and deep;
see here your own beauty rippling.

7: The Chariot

Like a mighty engine throbbing,
pistons counter-thrusting within steel,
our worlds are driven by
their opposites within.

Cock jays perch in opposite trees
and shout their individual song:
"I say, keep away !"
One living world is made.

The engine, armored centaur, heaves.
Upon its flank an emblem of its
government proclaims:
"I say, keep away !"

Split, we feel a master in our selves,
a governor in a bastion tower who
hoards up goods and keeps
a watch fire warm.

With rumbling gear inside of gear,
the turret and the cannon scan
beyond the border,
beyond our land.

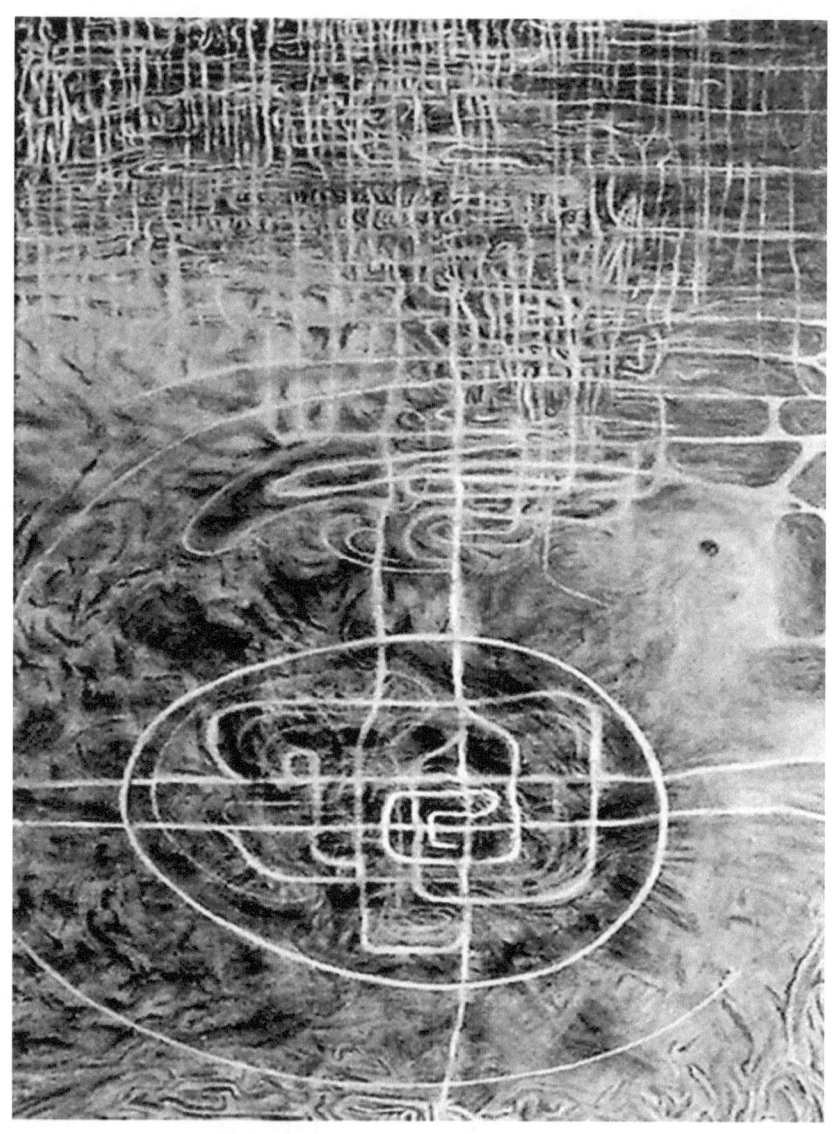

"Sacred Geometry"
Digitally modified photo of a detail
from the canvas painting "Earth Dragons"
by SR

8: Strength

Raindrop
      hanging still
      from a leaf tip
      knows
      the mighty tug
        of
        Earth
        and yet
      moves
      not.

The filaments
of liquid crystal
knitting it,
pure star stuff,
have
their own way.

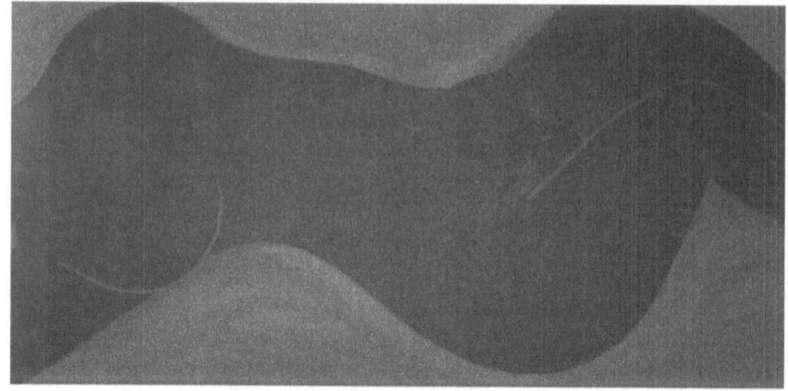

"So Dream Of Being Earth"
Painting on canvas by SR

9: The Hermit

Oh master of the high pass,
priest of the scouring wind
which keens among my bones,
reach down your knotty staff unto my grasp
that I may climb;
hold high that glorious lamp to show
my feet the stony way
and raise a song to greet
your long-forbidden love.

It was your song which drew me out,
which echoed through my heart and soul,
a faint high thrill to which my body chimed;
so up from the master's pillow jerked my head
and out from the castle cloister flew my feet
till here at last before you now I stand,
trembling and childlike, in your silence,
and pray you to caress me once again.

Why don't you sing? Why don't you sound the pipes?
Why don't you toss aside that cloak, that spectral mien,
and clasp me to your bosom with a hearty laugh?
Why now at long last chill and numbing silence?

Within the shadowy hood which blacks your radiant face
I do perceive half-lidded eyes which hint forbearance
and a tight-lipped little smile which answers: "Go !"

Bereft and yet obedient still, I turn away and blink aside
the tears to spy my barren home so far below.

And yet behold !
The wind has laid down to a murmuring sigh
and somehow, through your magic charm,
the waste I go to tread has turned to sparkling jewels
and to gold.

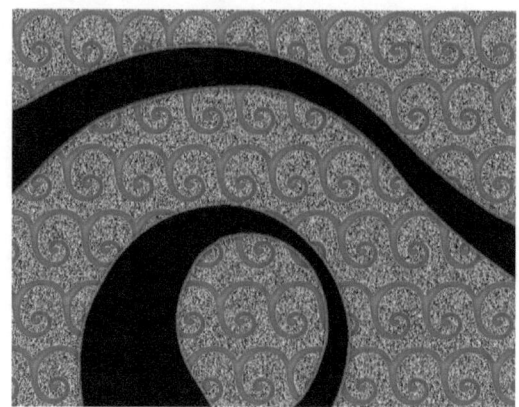

"A Sailor's True Tale"
Digital image based on
a canvas painting by SR

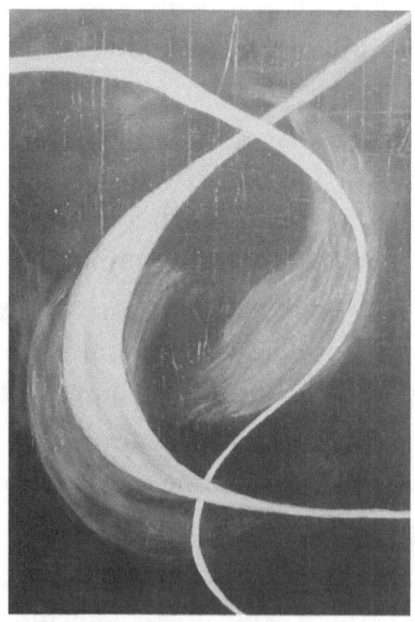

"Tide Of The Forest"
Painting on canvas by SR

10: The Wheel Of Fortune

Tumbling headlong with its next step, the great animal plunges through a matted screen which hid the tunnel mouth and down to the cave floor below.

Plunged from dusk into night, but bred to a forager's quick wit, it casts a glance about to see what light is shed by the hole it fell through.

Suddenly landed in a new place, it pulls itself up now to a comfortable squat and, being one of the laughing apes, grins back at its own breathless fall.

11: Justice

The firefly, tragically struggling,
sheds her phosphorescent glow upon
prismatic drops of spider glue which
a patient hunter hopes may hold her fast.

Here in a meadow in a wood on a plain,
now on this first night when all the suns
and moons together call her kind up
from a long waiting winter sleep
in the earth;

Now on this first night of love,
of life within the soaring phantom body
of a swarm of light, she has cast herself
into a net of jewels and hangs suspended,
half terrorized, half reconciled to fate.

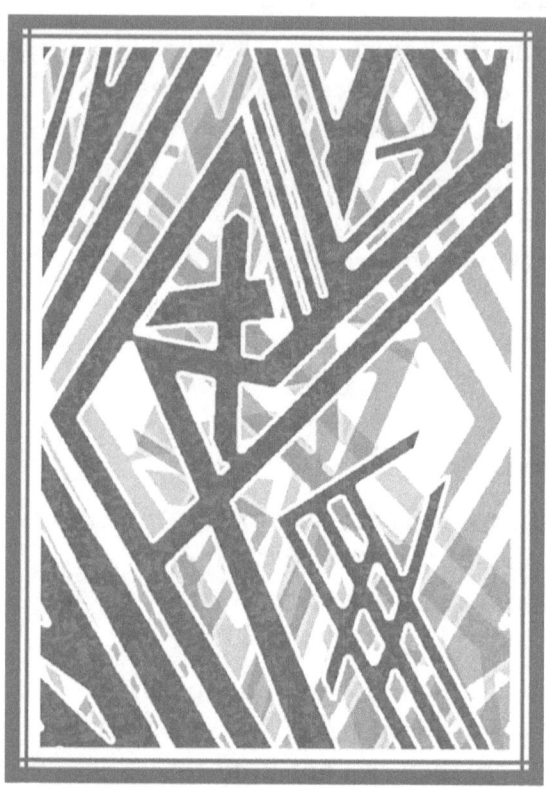

"Attributions Of The Minor Arcana
In Spirit Hill Tarot"
Digital image based on
a canvas painting by SR

12: The Hanged Man

~~~~~~~~~~~~~~~~~~~~~~~~~~~~~~~~
! Look ye with true eyes heavenward !
Behold:
! !

! !

** The Chariot Of A God **
! !

! !

this infinite-faceted jewel,
crystalline dream spindle,
heaven-spanning diadem of the god:
! !

! !

** Infinitude **
! !

! !

bridge between all stars,
from which I,
! !

! !

** A Priest **
! !

! !

descend.
~~~~~

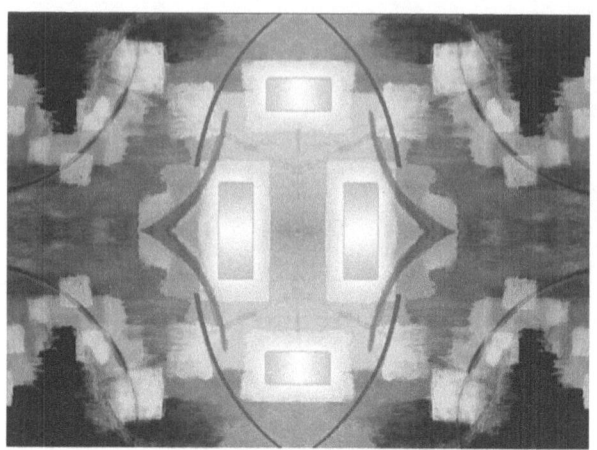

"Rebirth Of Courage"
Digital image based on
a canvas painting by SR

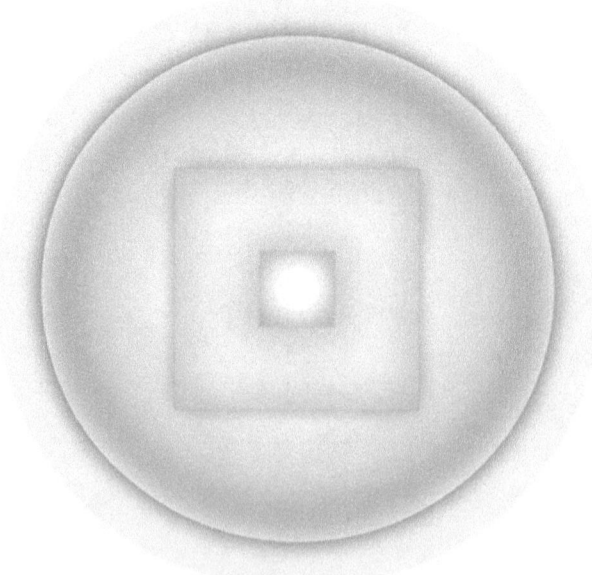

"The Soul's True Yearning"
Digital image by SR

13: Death

Youth is tenuous memory and
old age looms a fantasy somewhere;
room by room in a spiral hall
I walk the land.

What dread surrounds that door ahead !
What dreams lie there? What friend
or beast turns ear to the distant
measure of my tread?

14: Temperance

Water, blood of the earth,
come wash the poison from my flesh
and bring back life !

I dwelt with the others and thus
became thus;
now I give my self to you.

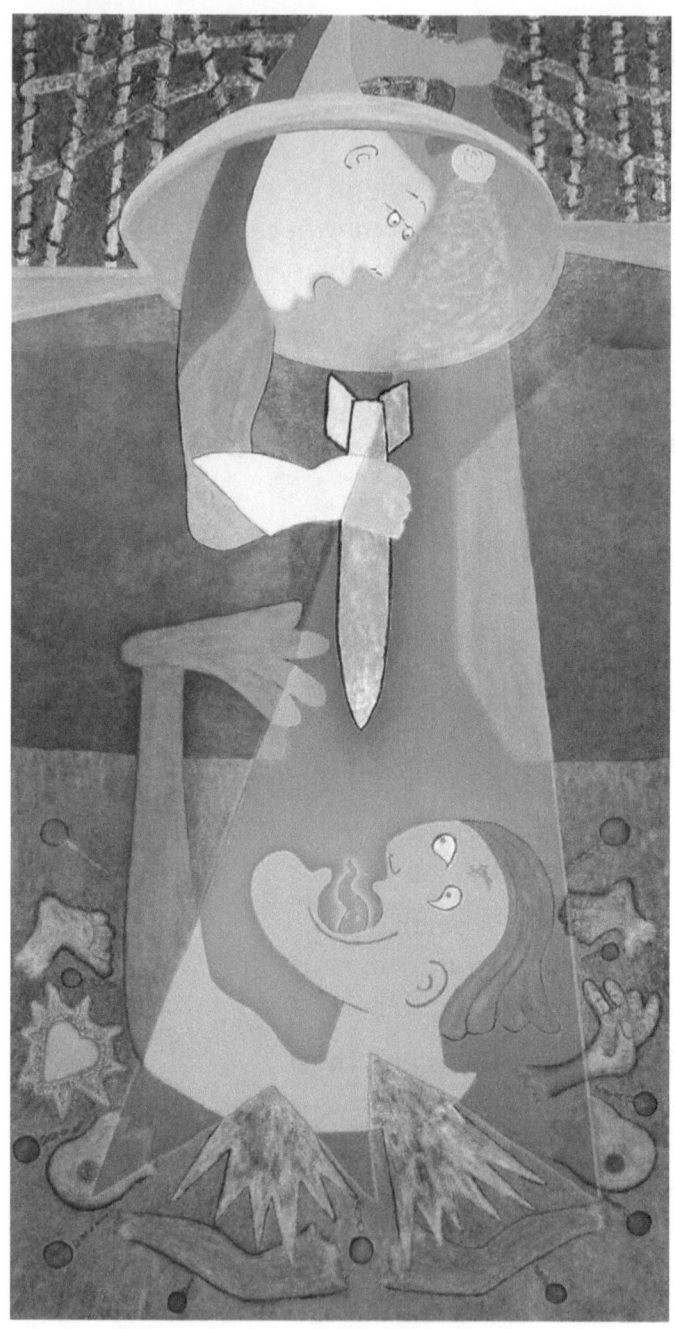

"Drone Strike In North Waziristan"
Painting on canvas by Stone Riley
On the web: www.stoneriley.com/dronestrike

15: The Devil

A living creature crushed
beneath a hero's thumb.
Seething hunger moist
on lips and tongue.

A writhing knotty snake within,
if not on constant victory fed,
will climb up on the hero's spine
and pluck his heart instead.

By stealth or dare he feeds the beast,
each morsel meaning he lives still.
He is too strong to sacrifice
that scabrous fruit of will.

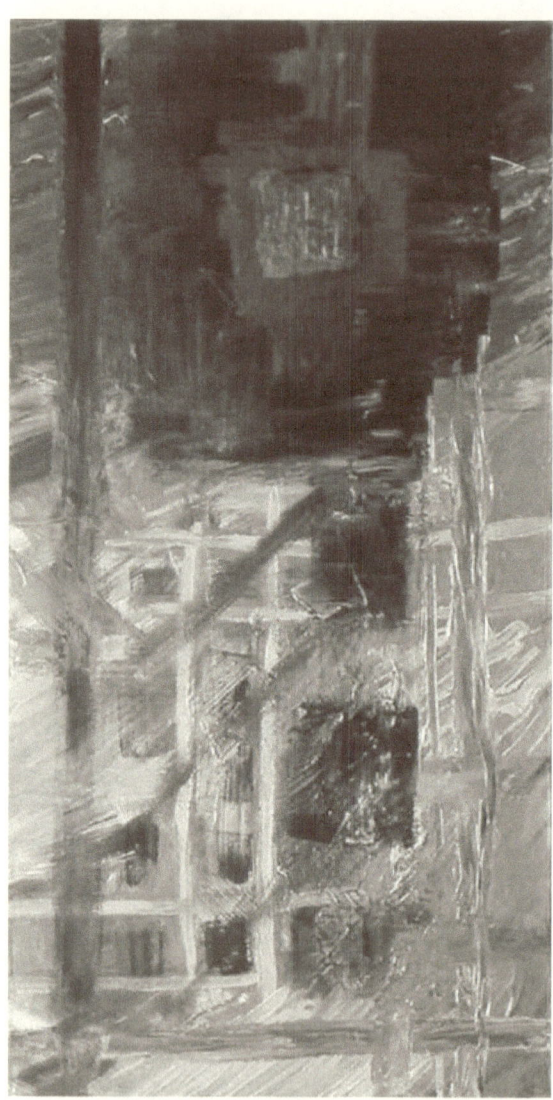

"Ghost In The Machine"
Painting on canvas by SR

16: The Tower

Upon this precipice built he a tower
to rule from high rich Eden's bower;
he fled the eye of God to cower,
to hoard up wife and goods and gear.

Spoke Fate:
"In brittle silence sit you here,
 in age-long soul-deep hate and fear,
 all for the sake of goods and gear,
 and jealousy of love."

"Stand off !" cried Adam to the dove,
"Repeat my mortal boast above:
 I am a man ! Earth's pulse shall move
 beneath the tapping of my thumb !"

But thunder rolls from God's great drum,
the gale and wave and earthquake come,
with ripening time all strivings sum,
and every fortress finds its hour.

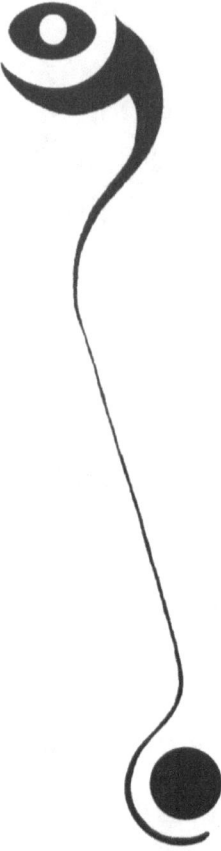

"An Eagle's Mighty Flight"
Digital image based on
a canvas painting by SR

17: The Star

Breaker waves 'neath lowering cloud
of autumn, driven by an icy wind;
here I stand transfixed with longing
on the shore of Skysealand.

Human eye drawn always outward
stretches forth the human hand
toward ever distant grey horizons
where the elements all blend.

Cold the heart and cold the soul,
cold the marrow in the bones does grow;
the yearning eye knows what to seek
but is the dogged flesh too weak?

Where is the rescue promised me?
How can my swooning heart yet come to be
a vessel of white light and sanctity
when all is dark and far from God's humanity?

A light !

Thank God, upon that distant curve
of blackening sea, at last a light !
So here I stand and through the eye
that piercing light darts to my soul
and there explodes into prismatic glow,
suffusing all.

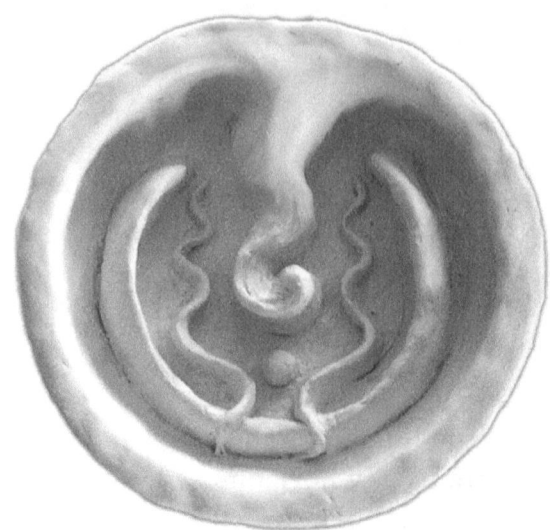

"Blessings"
Polymer clay sculpture by SR

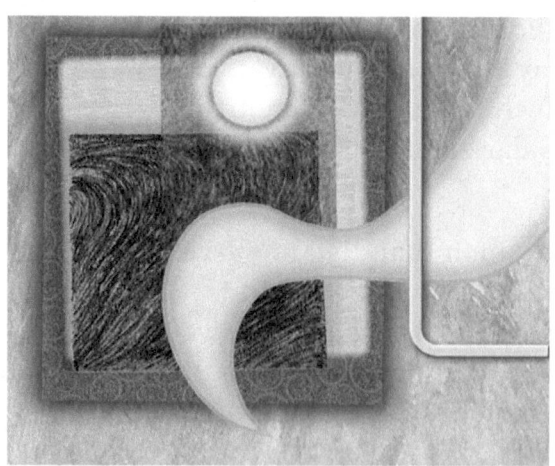

"Catsong"
Digital collage using various paintings
and drawings by SR

18: The Moon

Whispering shadow on my pillow lay.
(Arise ! Barefoot ! No robe ! Away !)
"How far the chase tonight?" I say.
The moonlight never answered.

19: The Sun

Soaked with the cold blind night, I stumble,
blunted sword in hand, panting,
not even breath enough for prayer,
my charges huddled in the broken circling wall
not knowing where the next attack may come.

But children of two eternal ones are we;
He whose word is fire
and She whose breast is clay.

Oh glorious mighty SOL !
The first ray of Your rising
pierced me and my heart flew up
to suck Your breath of flame !

You kiss me as You kiss the mother Earth
and bring back mighty life !
I thrust down roots into Her breast
and turn my face to you.

A circling temple from the broken stones
with altars male and female I heap up;
thereon this precious incense now I burn
to welcome You.

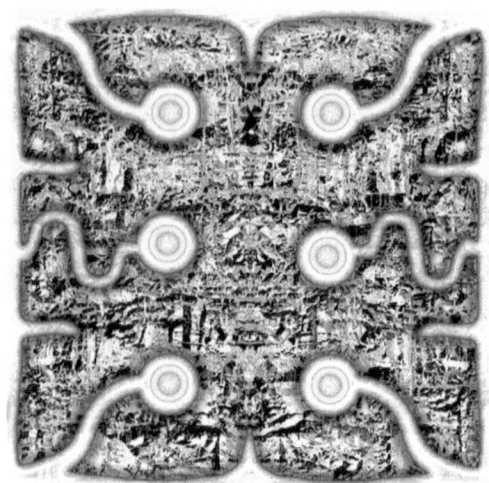

"Druid Chat"
Digitally modified canvas painting
by SR

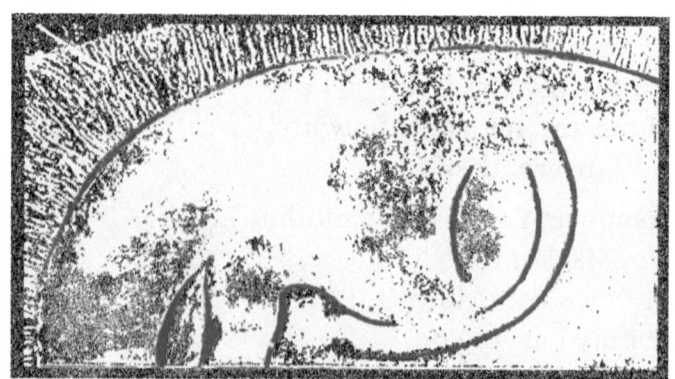

"You"
Digitally modified detail from
a canvas painting by SR

20: Judgment

Maze walker,
creature of a million colored chambers,
creature with a million colored patterns in your eye,
long ago lost here, almost guideless,
almost friendless, guessing every turn,
your steps have crossed a million beckoning portals,
tramped a million halls.

Now a new eye opens,
the eye above your self, holding no patterns, and sees:
the foot and floor, the patterned walls, light dancing to
the counter-patterned eye; now all is one !

A dance of all reality, of great and small infinity,
whose tiny steps and boundless whirls make up
yourself,
all that there is.

Now see the truth of All:
All is one thing, a world of self-same strangers,
cable of many threads,
garden of night and noon and morning,
magic loom of all there is.

21: The World

Unbounded parkland;
where the master gardener passes
exotic seeds flame
into great maturity.

Of course
the weathered lips reveal a smile;
all a wish could name
is here today.

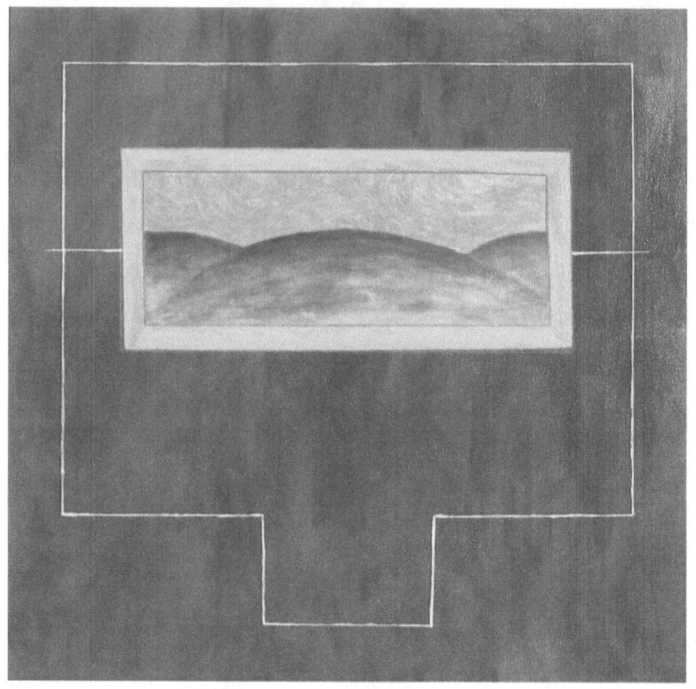

"Study On Matisse's Red Studio"
Painting on canvas by SR

Opening To Compassion

How often has a human caught the glittering eyes of fox or mouse or deer or bear or lion in the teeming forest or the grassy plain and - with a shudder or in sudden awesome ecstasy - they have felt everything outside themselves look into their being?

How often have the voices of the wind told someone that the spirits of the land are watching?

How often has the twinkling light of stars stabbed deep into a human soul?

How often has that penetration opened darkened places to the light of understanding so wisdom could begin, or broken through the hardened layers of a wounded heart so it might love again?

That is compassion.

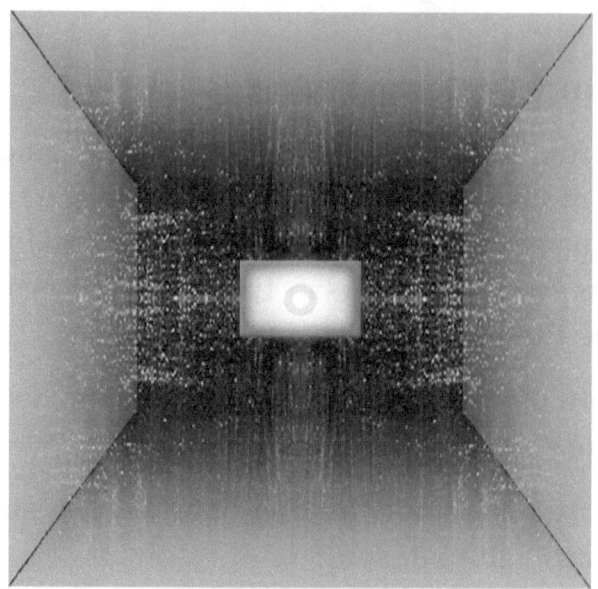

"Persephone's Gate"
Digital image by SR

August Evening

We are not imprisoned in ourselves and we are not alone. Your soul is not a single seed isolate in frozen ground nor is your heart a stone. No one can put up castle walls to hold themselves with any lock and key, for we are creatures of a teeming world.

Though we at times may fear the overawing beauty of a sunset or a dawn, the foreign eyes which penetrate our eyes, the grip of birdsong on our throat, the touch of whispering wind on naked cheek; though we at times may fear the loosening of the knotted strings of individual identity these intimate invasions bring, still soul beyond your soul is everywhere and crowding close.

Sit in company with a weeping woman, sharing grief for her beloved gone beyond the veil, and then up on the picture screen inside your eyes behold a presence standing right there beside the woman's shoulder in an aureole of other-light, presenting emblems of some sort about some message they would have you speak. Will you belie your claims of courage?
You will not.

So turn an ear to seek a whisper from the very depths of mystery, and study carefully and breathe and speak.

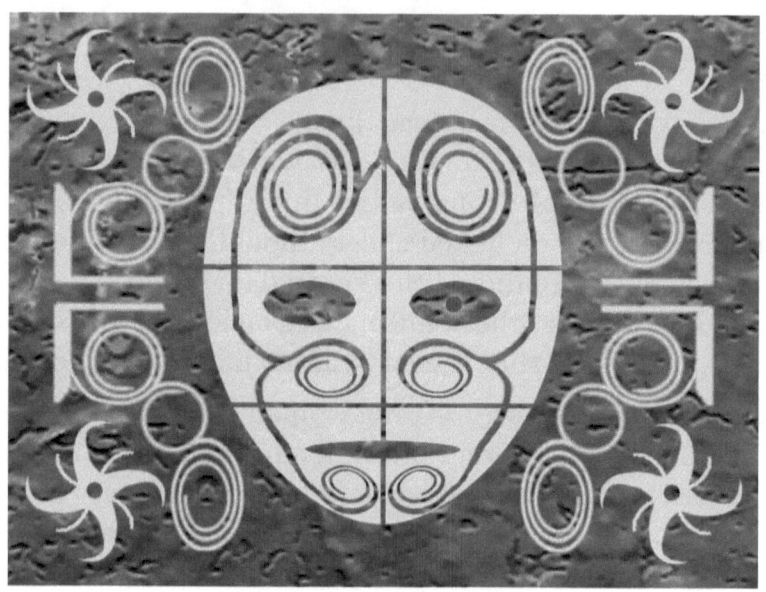

"Telling The Tale"
Digital image by SR

Songs Of Heroes

An old blind man up by the table's head
rises carefully to stand on wobbling legs.

Some good girls and boys assist
this blind old gentleman
to find the chair that some have run
to set in a shady spot beneath a tree.

Our local champion poet brings
the painted harp and gives it,
bowing by his knee.

And so he strikes the first note on the strings.
He begins to sing amid the ringing chime.
This reedy thinning voice cries out the tale
of great Odysseus who came home.

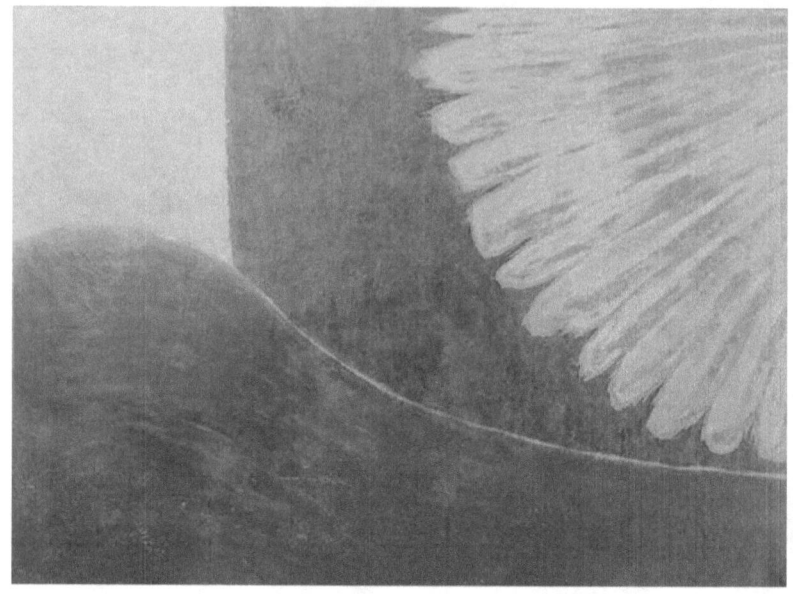

"Young Man At The Precipice"
Painting on canvas by SR

Journey To The West

Love is not the thing, nor hate.
Hope is not the mouse's scurrying feet and owl's sharp
beak, no more than these are fear.
What is the purpose of the poppy's fate then, or the logic
of my heart blood's heat, or yet the celestial motive of the
sky's Great Bear?
How do we live?
Why has the Cosmos brought us here?

When I was full of hope, I thought that was the
beginning and end of all things.
Then, full of yearning to be loved, I dreamed love was the
wellspring of delight.
But then, immersed in deep despair, I chose to live this
life for purposes that were far too obscured in smoke and
flame for me to know and name.
Why did I, in that dark hour, choose to live this life?
Why did I not yet fly away?

Love is not the thing, nor hate.
Faith is not the prisoner's chain, nor doubt the prophet's
holy flame, nor greed the mother's teat touched to the
sleeping baby's lips, nor is blessed charity the tyrant's grip.
All this is life, but what is life?
What is the melting of all opposites?

There is a man I truly hate; there is a woman whom I love.
That man is dead as he once wished for me, the woman
never met although my eyes search through the worlds
for only she.
Where is this woman who'll return my glance?
Where is that ancient foeman now when in my hands I
hold his broken blunted lance?
And where am I?

Where is this land wherein I stand alone?
What is this place? Is this my home?
I simply call this place my Skysealand.

One year when I was young and starting out across this
continent, I strained my eyes to look ahead to map the way.
That year, each Monday I would take a poem from an
ancient wisdom book and I would fold up the coded
rhyming wisdom neatly into my purse.
Then for seven days I'd search the curving trunk of every
tree and every mottled turtle's shell that I might pass
beside the way for explications written there by unseen
hands for me.
Well, the Gods were generous and kindly gave some of
their secrets up, but the boy I was then did not know
their language well.

An eagle's mighty flight; a turtle shell; amid the lovely
ripples of a brook, the various colored pebbles very
artfully arranged;
I made the best of it I could.
Indeed, several turnings of the way and crossroads were
very helpfully pointed out to me in advance by these
magic signs.
But now I've come a good way further on and, even
though the sunlight and the stars and meadow flowers
and hills and snow now all sing and whisper to me
audibly;
and even though the web of jewels of which all things are
made stands manifest and visible and palpable to my
fingers; yet even so,
more hidden secrets still remain.

Buddha says that all is bliss.
Solomon recommends a carefully considered trust.
Christ says you should take his word on faith.
Ganesh and Krishna both respectfully suggest that you
can dance your life with happy grace.

But for me, Merlin stands with a lantern held high in his hand,
leaning on a wooden staff up on a windy mountain top.
That wind blows down to gently touch my face and it
speaks to me in a woman's voice and all she says is just:
"Come."

No, love is not the thing, nor hate; not victory nor defeat.
Whatever guides my fate, whatever it may be that lures me on,
whatever it may be,
it is not anything that I can know so as to name.

Don't Stop Walking

Don't stop walking when
there is no way ahead.
      Your walking makes the path.
            The place you started from
            was cleared by others
                  and others will soon follow you
                      and pass and step ahead.

Text on the picture: When you confront reality with your whole being, your work becomes mysticism and your life becomes myth.

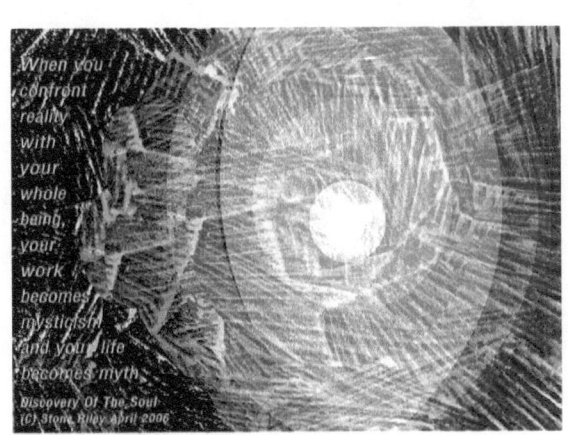

"Discovery Of The Soul"
Digital image by SR

Components
: A Detail Cross Reference List

Document #3

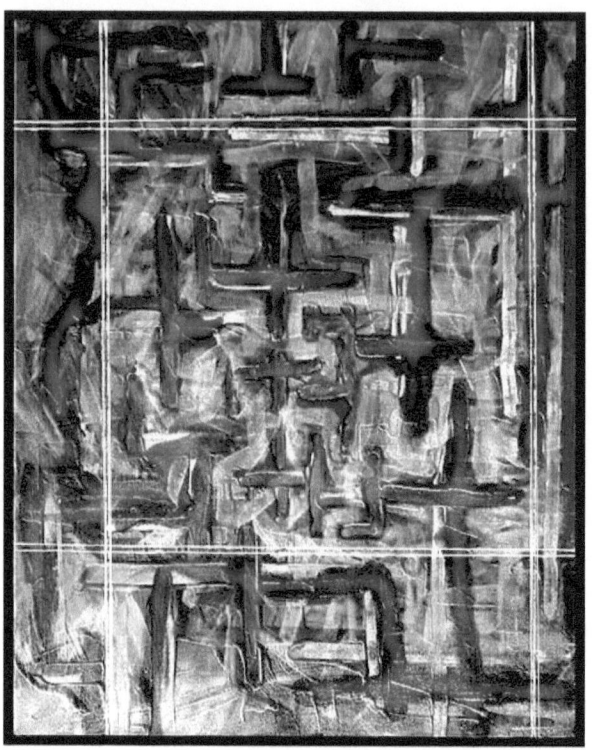

"The Look In Andy's Eyes"
Painting on canvas by SR

Components:
A Detail Cross Reference List
(Document #3)

> Overview

Here is a detailed cross-referenced list of the cards in Simple Tarot and Spirit Hill Tarot.

Revision July 2015: Please ignore this section!! Some good readers whom I love report bewilderment with this. Please skip through to the next document!! This is a technical data listing from my Tarot information processing project and it is here only because I try to be a good technician. This listing is probably not important or interesting for you.

This shows each card's bit of poetry, composed for Simple Tarot 35 years ago then carried to the other deck's first edition 10 years ago.

Alright, thinking on it, I'm also imitating old occult books by putting this here, the alchemists' diaries of their experimental results (very puzzling) and such as that. So maybe this is meant for you (you in particular) to read. But probably not.

For Spirit Hill cards here is also given the title and materials of the painting, sculpture or photograph from which the card's picture was digitally wrought, plus a note on those for which Zoe Salmon has collaboration credit. This data is not given for the Simple Tarot cards because they bear unique little pencil drawings.

Attentive scholars (if any such are ever reading this) will notice that most of the Minor Arcana follows the old alchemical equation of Swords = Air; Coins = Earth; Wands =

Fire; Cups = Water. (The Simple has the classic tools while Spirit Hill has elements.) However, the newer scheme of Swords = Fire and Wands = Air, which appeared during my time, is used among the Aces.

Also there are important changes of meaning between the two decks in the wording on these cards: Tens of Coins & Earth, Sixes of Wands & Fire, High Priest, Hermit, Devil. The Fool has a wording change that either is or is not consequential.

Most pictures in the Spirit Hill are crafted from paintings but these are from photos: Ten Of Wands, Knight Of Earth and these are from sculptures: Two Of Wands, Eight of Earth. Also, in Spirit Hill Major Arcana most paintings were made especially for their card but for these cards the painting preexisted: High Priestess, High Priest, Strength.

Please don't ask me to explain these inconsistencies, or to draw some philosophical conclusions of some sort, for I could only guess. The 35-year process that this work created for itself created the data shown here too. I performed its operations and observed.

I must tell you: These decks are vastly indebted to the extraordinary Wilhelm - Baines edition of China's great immortal classic I Ching. (The edition with its sunny yellow cover hidden in a gray paper wrap.) That great book's semi-haiku poetic style inspired all the little poems on my cards while the book's mental images were projecting the Simple Tarot's drawings in my eyes.

And of course my grateful mention of "a turtle's shell" in the Tarot poem Journey To The West obviously refers to the I Ching also.

My beloved partner Zoe Salmon was collaborator on several of the paintings, as noted here below. She made the smiles on "Shrine of Ishtar" and "Goddess Of The Witches" and also made a smiling photo portrait that appears on the Knight Of Earth. Much much more of this will be told in a later document in this series called "The Fig Tree".

> The Minor Arcana Cards

Ace Of Swords (Simple Tarot)
Poem: Force, the block is split, a new thing can emerge.

Ace Of Air (Spirit Hill Tarot)
Poem: The enterprise begins.
From painting on canvas: Seagull Turning

Ace Of Coins or Earth (Both decks)
Poem: Good fortune, success in the world's pursuits.
From painting on canvas: View From Hubble

Ace Of Wands (Simple Tarot)
Poem: Strength, energy, the enterprise begins.

Ace Of Fire (Spirit Hill Tarot)
Poem: A new thing can emerge.
From painting on canvas: Island Of Time

Ace Of Cups or Water (Both decks)
Poem: Fertility, beauty, pleasure.
From painting on canvas: Awaking In A Dream

Two Of Swords or Air (Both decks)
Poem: Balanced force, indecision, a kind of comradeship.
From sculpture: Uther In Prayer

Two Of Coins or Earth (Both decks)
Poem: Change, but harmony remains.
From painting on canvas: San Diego Bay

Two of Wands or Fire (Both decks)
Poem: If one desires, another will obey, yet little joy lies with them.
From a magazine illustration based on a painting: Antigone

Two Of Cups or Water (Both decks)
Poem: Accept & receive, invite & join, love & be loved.
From painting on canvas: Persephone's Gate

Three Of Swords or Air (Both decks)
Poem: Catastrophe; the bonds of the human heart are burst.
From painting on canvas: The Agony Of Love

Three Of Coins or Earth (Both decks)
Poem: Material increase.
From painting on canvas: Islands Of Dream

Three of Wands or Fire (Both decks)
Poem: Fruitful partnership.
From painting on canvas: Portrait Of Gauguin

Three Of Cups or Water (Both decks)
Poem: Hail Fortune which grants a perfect outcome.
From painting on canvas: Pensacola Bay

Four of Swords or Air (Both decks)
Poem: Power regains itself in exile.
From painting on canvas: Phoenix

Four Of Coins or Earth (Both decks)
Poem: The owner, and his power, and his love of power.
From painting on canvas: Calliope

Four of Wands or Fire (Both decks)
Poem: Competence so perfect it seems like a natural flow.
From painting on assembled wood: Chop Wood Carry Water

Four Of Cups or Water (Both decks)
Poem: Joy, where are you? Pleasure, love where are you?
Loneliness.
From painting on canvas: Lost Child

Five of Swords or Air (Both decks)
Poem: Honor stands shattered; real self is exposed.
From painting on canvas: John The Baptist

Five Of Coins or Earth (Both decks)
Poem: Impoverished loneliness.
From painting on canvas: Memory Of Veronica

Five of Wands or Fire (Both decks)
Poem: A storm of competition, this is the law.
From painting on canvas: Reality

Five Of Cups or Water (Both decks)
Poem: Good comes often in disguises, not what was hoped.
From painting on canvas: The Search For God

Six of Swords or Air (Both decks)
Poem: With aid, the end comes in view.
From painting on canvas: Tolkien

Six Of Coins or Earth (Both decks)
Poem: Success and generosity.
From painting on canvas: Xanadu

Six of Wands (Simple Tarot)
Poem: Feet tap the Earth's sea, a heart beats, beyond, a god sings.

Six of Fire (Spirit Hill Tarot)
Poem: Feet tap the Earth's sea, a heart beats, beyond, a goddess sings.
From painting on canvas: Portrait Of Beven #1

Six Of Cups or Water (Both decks)
Poem: The past speaks.
From painting on canvas: House Of The Spirits

Seven of Swords or Air (Both decks)
Poem: Hopes and schemes, partial success but fear.
From painting on canvas: Forsythia [A collaboration with Zoe Salmon.]

Seven Of Coins or Earth (Both decks)
Poem: Delay but growth.
From painting on canvas: Lunar Animus

Seven of Wands or Fire (Both decks)
Poem: Breaking through at last.
From painting on assembled wood: Pulling The Mandrake Root

Seven Of Cups or Water (Both decks)
Poem: Strange visions and hopes, but insufficient will to make them real.
From painting on canvas: Off-Center Composition, 20th Century

Eight of Swords or Air (Both decks)
Poem: Seized by useless battle, bitter resentment.
From painting on canvas: World War One

Eight Of Coins or Earth (Both decks)
Poem: Smile, relax, for the driver is accustomed to control.
From sculpture: World Order Inc.

Eight of Wands or Fire *(Both decks)*
Poem: Great speed impelled by great desire.
From painting on canvas: Cornucopia

Eight Of Cups or Water (Both decks)
Poem: Turn from the light, welcome the loneliness, walk in doubt.
From painting on assembled canvas: The Ecstasy Of Saint Teresa [A collaboration with Zoe Salmon.]

Nine of Swords or Air (Both decks)
Poem: Despair and misery, for all seems lost.
From painting on assembled canvas and vinyl: Catherine The Great [A collaboration with Zoe Salmon.]

Nine Of Coins or Earth (Both decks)
Poem: Financial security, accomplishments, certainty.
From painting on canvas: Mycenae

Nine of Wands or Fire (Both decks)
Poem: Life, subtle and vigorous, denies all obstacles.
From painting on canvas: Poppy

Nine Of Cups or Water (Both decks)
Poem: Body, passion, intellect, soul, all in harmony.
From painting on canvas: Einstein's God

Ten of Swords or Air (Both decks)
Poem: The desolate ruin of past delusion.
From painting on canvas: Minotaur

Ten Of Coins (Simple Tarot)
Poem: Family gifts – wonderful perhaps, but shaped by the giver's need.

Ten Of Earth (Spirit Hill Tarot)
Poem: Sacrifice for family and friends.
From painting on canvas: Earth Dragons

Ten of Wands or Fire (Both decks)
Poem: The empty cathedral: erected in doubt, echoing with guilt
From Digital photograph: Through A Small Window

Ten Of Cups or Water (Both decks)
Poem: Perfect love and friendship, attainment of the human heart's desire.
From painting on canvas: Universal Dance

Page of Swords or Air (Both decks)
Poem: The young cadet: proven but jealous of his prizes.
From painting on canvas: The God At Noon

Page Of Coins or Earth (Both decks)
Poem: The serious scholar can argue any point.
From a design drawing for a painting on assembled canvas and wood: Corridors [A collaboration with Zoe Salmon.]

Page of Wands or Fire (Both decks)
Poem: The leopard's cub, all brilliant speed, a messenger.
From painting on wood: Sun In Her Hair #2

Page Of Cups or Water (Both decks)
Poem: Philosopher, poet, child of the ancient Greeks, fond of justice.
From painting on canvas: The Poet's Craft

Knight of Swords or Air (Both decks)
Poem: Calculated fury.
From painting on canvas: The Search For Freedom

Knight Of Coins (Simple Tarot)
Poem: Hard working, he depends upon his skills.

Knight Of Earth (Spirit Hill Tarot)
Poem: Loyal, striving, he depends upon his skills.
From digital photograph: Photo of Stone Riley by Zoe Salmon

Knight of Wands or Fire (Both decks)
Poem: Charming, attractive, ready to gallop.
From painting on canvas: The Seasons

Knight Of Cups or Water (Both decks)
Poem: Oh sweet seducer, melody of youth.
From painting on assembled canvas and wood: Swan At Moonrise

Queen of Swords or Air (Both decks)
Poem: A vibrant woman dressed in mourning.
From painting on canvas: Woman On Main Street

Queen Of Coins or Earth (Both decks)
Poem: A magnificent woman – confident, perceptive, generous
– or an untrustworthy man.
From painting on canvas card: Poem # 1

Queen of Wands or Fire (Both decks)
Poem: Patroness of female honor and human family warmth.
From painting on canvas: Lady Of The Witches
[A collaboration with Zoe Salmon.]

Queen Of Cups or Water (Both decks)
Poem: Fear this voice and despair, welcome it and learn.
From painting on canvas: Gorgon

King of Swords or Air (Both decks)
Poem: Commander of great forces, marching.
From painting on canvas: Uther In Victory

King Of Coins or Earth (Both decks)
Poem: Simple, profound direct decisions and self-deceit.
From painting on canvas: Green Man

King Of Wands (Simple Tarot)
Poem: A grand old man today.

King Of Fire (Spirit Hill Tarot)
Poem: A fine old man today.
From painting on assembled canvas: The Blessed Head Of Bran

King Of Cups or Water *(Both decks)*
Poem: The paragon of animals; he stands like an angel and speaks like a god.
From painting on canvas: Buddha Of Infinite Compassion

> The Major Arcana Cards

0: The Fool (Simple Tarot)
Poem: Glory! Glory! Glory!

0: The Fool (Spirit Hill Tarot)
Poem: Glory! Glory! Glory! Glory!
From painting on canvas: The Fool

1: The Magician (Both decks)
Poem: We absorb the force of Nature and release it as we judge fit.
From painting on canvas: The Magician

2: The High Priestess (Both decks)
Poem: A thin veil billows at the borders of our land; infinity is hidden and revealed.
From painting on canvas: Shrine Of Ishtar Beneath Jerusalem's City Wall [A collaboration with Zoe Salmon.]

3: The Empress (Both decks)
Poem: The ancient mother of our race was called the giver of all things.
From painting on canvas: The Empress

4: The Emperor (Both decks)
Poem: The ancient father of our race was called the maker of all names.
From painting on canvas: The Emperor

5: The High Priest (Simple Tarot)
Poem: We honor the governor who sees infinity and teaches truth.

5: The High Priest (Spirit Hill Tarot)
Poem: We honor the teacher who sees infinity and teaches truth.
From painting on canvas: Shadowland # 3

6: The Lovers (Both decks)
Poem: Through a veil our longing kiss, then hard choices & compromises; we must know & become each other.
From painting on canvas: The Lovers

7: The Chariot (Both decks)
Poem: I and you, with and without, dare and dare not; such words provide our power in this world.
From painting on canvas: The Chariot

8: Strength (Both decks)
Poem: Cleanly United, we shine within.
From painting on canvas: Horus Is Conceived

9: The Hermit (Simple Tarot)
Poem: Worlds touch, we are moved.

9: The Hermit (Spirit Hill Tarot)
Poem: Alone, we watch and hope for life.
From painting on canvas: The Hermit

10: The Wheel Of Fortune (Both decks)
Poem: Having nought else, we trust to luck.
From painting on canvas: The Wheel Of Fortune

11: Justice (Both decks)
Poem: Knot by knot, we weave perfection.
From painting on canvas: Justice

12: The Hanged Man (Both decks)
Poem: Immersed in a world of reflections, we hang on a cord of truth.
From painting on canvas: The Hanged Man

13: Death (Both decks)
Poem: Our lives wither and bloom, memory scarcely lingers.
From painting on canvas: Death

14: Temperance (Both decks)
Poem: Rushing from the height of passion against the hard Earth of reality, we find the stillness.
From painting on canvas: Temperance

15: The Devil (Simple Tarot)
Poem: Will can nearly make us gods.

15: The Devil (Spirit Hill Tarot)
Poem: We hide our wish to serve our will.
From painting on canvas: The Devil

16: The Tower (Both decks)
Poem: Our will is folly.
From painting on canvas: The Tower

17: The Star (Both decks)
Poem: Prismatic, we burst from a core of truth.
From painting on canvas: The Star

18: The Moon (Both decks)
Poem: Intrigued, fearful, hopeful and enraptured, we proceed as though into the past.
From painting on canvas: The Moon

19: The Sun (Both decks)
Poem: Gates thrown open, we greet the vanquisher of night.
From painting on canvas: The Sun

20: Judgment (Both decks)
Poem: Our raveled threads will all combine.
From painting on canvas: Fall Of The Jade Emperor

21: The World (Both decks)
Poem: Our lives, the limbs and twigs and leaves of the great life.
From painting on canvas: The World

Particular Advice
For The Technician

Document #4

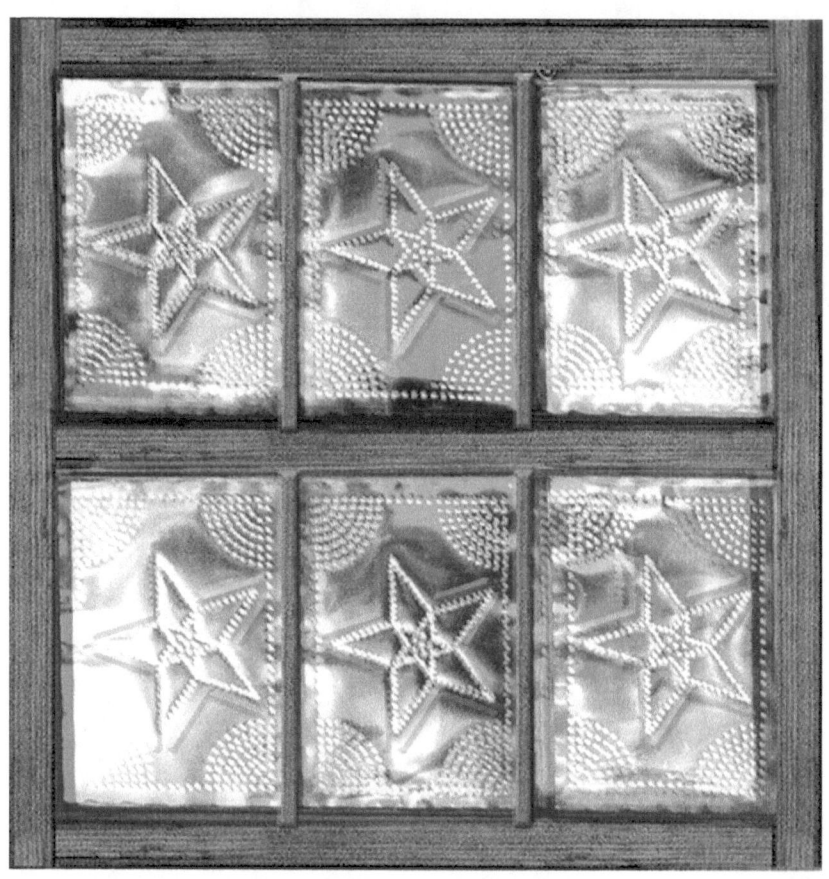

"The Substance Of Reality"
Digital photo montage by SR

Particular Advice For The Technician
(Document #4)

> Objective

Worldwide merciless robber bands, proclaiming funda-
mentalist faith in Capitalism, are attacking We The People
while we search desperately for a safe home on this belea-
guered planet. That's a movie in our mind's eyes, projected
outward by our words and actions and inward by our
expectations.

The heroic mode of life – knowing the world is true,
knowing you can help, letting difficulties teach you – can
give us work and love and joy but we don't know yet if that
strategy can save the world and give us safety. Still, we
struggle on against the forces of insanity and death because
we must, not because there is some chance of victory.

So goes the desperately heroic story we are playing.
And we get plenty of supporting action from our enemies
when we play it.

But what if we had more vision? What if we could look
into the world and see reality outside current imaginings?
What if we could look inside our own projection booth to
change the settings? What if we had some piece of strange
technology to let us really see each other and ourselves?
Could we find more creativity? If we knew each other better could we be more like kin, cooperate solidly in what
must be done and thereby simply win?

We must arise in solid confident consensus to over-
whelmingly enforce reality's demands. To me, an artist

engineer, this sounds like we need some kind of pocket size commonplace hand held tool, some kind of scope and gauge and meter of the human mind and heart and soul. I think Tarot, and especially very beautiful Tarot, will help.

> But Surely This Is Nonsense?

I'm going to tell you a technology story.

Me and this other guy walk in a taco joint near work for lunch – this is on the factory side of a New England town near the wire mill – me with an ulterior motive in my jacket pocket.

It was summer 1999, 16 years ago. This other guy is smart but he's only got a one-week job doing just bulk coding in the wire factory's computer office. We all had the world-wide famous "Y2K" bug that year, which you might recall, and he's helping us with that. Me, I'm the regular software staff at that factory so for the one week he'll be there I am his coworker lead.

Now, all I've said is that I'd show him where to get some Mexican food but actually I have a private project. So after we eat I push the restaurant paper trash aside and pull my prototype out of my jacket pocket, slap it on the table.

A cardboard box: Ordinary cardboard brown but pocket size, a small unmarked box and there it is by itself alone equally between us on the table. He's not talkative anyway, and the poor guy is sad today, maybe depressed, he's feeling preoccupied and grim today for some reason, so he just looks at it for the moment until I begin my prepared remarks.

You see, I have chosen him to be a test subject.

And I said, "This is an art project. I'm an artist. I am asking people to take a look at it so I can watch their reactions."

That is such a peculiar thing to hear, and seems so harmless, that every person I asked accepted out of curiosity, as he now did, just a shrug however. Also, I was glad to see even a little light of joy in his face at the opportunity for entertainment.

So now my little recruiting thing's introduction: First I'm sure I told him, "Understand, this has no impact or relation to the job at all whatsoever." I'm sure I did that.

You understand I'm quoting accurately even now because it was a tried and true routine and because that run of it became one of the most important experiences of my art career.

It went like this: I'd lay down a very flat neutral tone like doing a survey on a street corner and I said: "I am an artist and this is a Chinese fortunetelling cookie kind of art project."

That's a good line and he actually smiles at the fortune cookie bit and finally commits himself to speaking out loud, but still just gives me "Okay."

So I continue to the next step, loosening my vocal tone for the important test instructions and the legalistic assurances:

"We have a simple procedure. Inside the box are 26 paper cards with writing on them. I will ask you to think of something, then ask you to open the box and pick any card at all, then read it silently while I watch. The project is at a very crucial early stage and I need to find out how it's doing. I will not ask for any personal information about you or your life whatsoever."

And my guy – he is a mid-level casual worker approaching middle age with faded office clothes and a low end car in the parking lot outside, at the center of an unhappy day for reasons I will never know and – largely for the entertainment value of it – he has chosen to take my peculiar project seriously.

He did not know how very serious I was about it. In fact, this unmarked box of 26 hand lettered cards was an ambitious daring effort and the latest step in my true life's work.

Example: One card in there has **"L is for Lake"** lettered boldly at the top. Then in normal print it tells a tiny seed of story, that one day you're walking in some hills, getting foot-sore and dusty, and you find a beautiful lake. It's quite isolated so of course you strip off and go in, discovering that while you're simply floating there your soul rises to the surface.

Here is a commonplace blue-ruled index card, hundred to a pack from an office supply store, hand lettered, no picture, but is secretly the Ace Of Water card from Tarot. It ends with a small seed of advice, supposed to be simultaneously spiritual and practical advice somehow, then finally repeats "L is for Lake".

That's only one example of what's in the box and I have no knowledge which this test subject picked, for there are 26 cards in there, A and Z and all the rest, and I will only see the blank backs of the cards in this test setup across a table.

But you've probably got the concept: This is supposed to be an alphabet of human life that an intelligent person could memorize and then throw away the physical cards, thereafter working up some other process for doing read-ings with no physical impedimenta at all.

It's supposed to be in case you're in a homeless camp or if you're after our modern world has crashed or what-ever. That's the concept. And of course human beings in many cultures develop tools of that general type.

Now my good gentleman has nodded that he's ready. In this moment I was here with you explaining that above, he has quickly and carefully thought about it. He has weigh-ed the likely entertainment value inherent in my claim of "art", has weighed this opportunity to help a stranger brother, has weighed my pledge to leave his privacy and livelihood alone, has weighed whatever thoughts he has on Chinese fortune cookies, and has accepted, so he nodded decisively for me to go ahead.

Now I offer him the exact same suggestion I offered you, on page 1 of Document #1 in this series where it says to choose some issue in your life where you genuinely want good advice or a hint of how to see things usefully and truly, and it tells you get your issue extremely clear and vivid in your mind. I tell him that.

Then I study his face. He is visibly a little cautious, finds some touchy problem in his life he is reluctant to think about so that he winces and frowns, but his eyes show me he is certainly thinking about that thing, and pausing to collect it vividly, and then he says to me, in pain you understand, "Yeah?"

"Now please," I answer, "if you want to do this, just open the little box and pick out any card and read it. Please read it silently to yourself."

With his hands trembling enough to see, he opens the box and takes a card out which he holds near himself, in some degree of privacy, to read. He's frowning in intense multi-layered focus.

May we talk technicalities?

After all, this small box is supposedly an information storage and retrieval device. Right? And this design problem is elegant, interesting and useful, is it not? Very elegant perhaps? So how about we dip into the technicalities of the design a little bit? Why don't I just take a minute to list my top 3 design objectives?

Okay? Design Objective #1 might surprise you. It surprised me when I first noticed it during my earlier work. It's this:

Since a questioner is allowed to ask absolutely any question about their life, a well functioning Tarot deck kind of system must contain a good answer to any possible human life question. And that is to say, the information in my device, if it were just sorted out in an appropriate way, could tell every human story.

Of course that sounds impossibly huge but it actually turns out that human life everywhere is uniform enough, and humans are so brilliant, that this Objective #1 is not even very hard.

Okay? Should I get even further in the technical weeds on this? Just for a minute I'll point this out: One essential feature of the data storage in this kind of device is beauty.

It is beautiful poetry in some of these systems. After all, we know that even a single phrase of poetry sometimes opens whole volumes of memory and imaginings in our minds. It's like some censoring part of our mind gets dazzled by the beauty and just lets poetry come in and open every associated door and then we can look in those compartments.

Okay then, there is a traditional practice in our culture you might be familiar with: For example in the U.S. South where I come from, among people who understand the Bible vividly, it is common to ask a question about life, then open a Bible and touch a page to find a wise appropriate answer. So which version of the Bible do they choose? In my experience people always use the King James Version. Its language is far more beautiful than other versions so it's far more evocative in your mind.

(Me too; In the King James I love especially Ecclesiastes and Job; this is fascinating non-Socratic philosophy poetry supposedly originally composed by Solomon and in the King James the thinking power is huge. I hold that entire book in very deep respect.)

But I don't have a box of beautiful poems waiting for us on the restaurant table. I am a fair poet sometimes but have never yet risen to the Shakespearean level of the King James. No, what I have inside that box – or at least what my design calls for in that box – is beautiful story.

I do know story pretty well. It has been the school and core of my artistic practice. I learned it by years of diligent performance.

We started in 1969, me and story, talking war resistance with fellow U.S. soldiers during an especially terrifying U.S. war, studying oratory tips in the Autobiography of Malcolm X on how to serve an audience in mortal stress like that. That was my first artistic discipline, as to say disciplined art work.

Then we got some polish from the storytelling boom of the 1970's and 80's. I joined a guild and the public came to our guild shows in droves. I got up to treatments of the great British and Greek stuff, had them jumping to their feet with that sometimes. Me and story learned to weave the spell quite beautifully in Pagan rituals too where the magic gets freaking bare naked.

So I have studied story. So for this new project's design – this project which has by now matured into the Alphabet-icon Tarot – I chose story as the mode of beauty in which human life wisdom would be coded.

One of those index cards tells that you're hiking in the hills and find a beautiful lake. Another says you're resting after giving birth. Another has you gazing at the stars while pondering life on Earth. Another says you bring a treasure home from a cruel land of giants while another has you bite an apple, taste its delicious juice and see the seeds. You're sitting waiting for a door to open in another.

Do you see that 26 of these could possibly, all together mixed and matched, tell every human story?

And of course, in our taco shop that noon – there with the poor wage slave who has become my good stranger brother gentleman – I am sitting there studying his face in pain and hoping ardently that a card sorted out of that box – or two or three cards if he wants – will offer real guidance by telling a true story of where he is, plus show an available path ahead to a good ending.

But before we slip back into that story – which, as I've already said, was one of the strongest experiences of my art career – before we return to that restaurant lunch, we really must discuss Design Objective #2. Because you are already asking about it.

So let's skip lots and lots of other technical stuff but I am sure you are already wanting to hear about Objective #2. And then later back there we will find the third objective.

Objective #2 is this: When our good friend's fingertips reach in that little box they definitely must find a card that is correct for his question. And of course you're asking me: How?

And my answer is: I do not know. When a human gets into a properly attentive willful and receptive state of mind, and if you're using a system of expression where you understand the language, then a correct card does turn up – or a correct spot on a correct page of a book will attract your eye or other such – or, if you're among the ancient Greeks, when you toss some pebbles on a board they will make a correct geometric pattern – reliably as if in conscious conversation with you. With my own eyes I've seen this happen several thousand times.

I know how it feels – anyone who does this knows how it feels, as you probably know too from mysterious creative moments in your life that were effectively similar – but I cannot explain it.

Alright, the obvious possibilities: This happens either by some illusion in our thinking, or by some surprising fact about time and space and all of that, or both. Me, I guess it's both. I guess this is a mental trick about memory and imagination, developed in us by evolution, involving quantum physics. Just please don't call this extremely vague hypothesis a "theory".

But I can offer some helpful context to this philosophical dilemma. I can, and this might make you feel better.

From ancient Greece, a fellow named Plato tells us stories about his dearly loved teacher Socrates.

In one, Plato has Socrates telling us a story about the time when he, Socrates, went around to all the best creative artists of his city, asking all of them the same question.

That was Athens in its golden age so they were surely poets and playwrights, maybe actors but maybe not, painters on pottery who were sculptors really too, the other sculptors who carved stone statues, maybe the painters of pictures on walls, and certainly some brilliant architects.

Plato says Socrates says he went around asking all of these highly creative people the same highly annoying question: Where did all of their creative stuff come from?

Well, Socrates says – or Plato says he says – they would all give the same easy answer first. Everyone of them – every one – first said, "Well, it comes from the Gods."

But that's too easy because nobody knows what the Gods are. So then, since Socrates was Socrates, he would press them. He would insist, "But really really really, where does all of the creative stuff come from?"

And every one of them, every one, would answer, "I don't know."

So if you ask me how does that vast creative moment happen when a human hand reaches for a Tarot card and knows which one to pick to tell a story true – and the moments in your life that are equally astonishing – and moments when a hand holds a sculpting chisel or a painting brush and finds the truth – then I feel in good company when I answer, "I don't know." But I certainly do know this and design to count on this: Human beings are brilliant.

Have you watched an artist weaving tapestry? Human life is a weaving together of threads. And we're very good at that.

We human beings are very often quick to drop one thread and pick up a different thread to twine into our life when reality demands it. We're very good at that, but of course to do that we must look beyond our current selves.

To choose new threads of life we need to look outside our fears and shames and pains, our current expectations and beliefs. So we constantly – all through human history all across the world – resort to vision equipment like Tarot.

So we have at last arrived back at our workman's lunch. My stranger friend, if I presume to call him that, sits beyond our restaurant table, and over there his hands and face – with our paper card in his hand like a theater prop – are enacting tight held silent drama. It is a drama that is real and real and real.

What did he ask? I do not know. What answer did the magic I have conjured for him then advise? I do not know.

But I can see thoughts across his face, thoughts reaching through the tiny gestures of his hands, turbulently flowing through him in the wave-like motion done by ocean water rising on a beach, and then of course it breaks:

He throws down that card, face down on the table there, and grabs the little box and reaches in it for another.

What card now? I do not know. But at least my greatest fear is answered, or seems to be, by his small surprise of recognition, then the smile of waking hope that plays across his face above the pain while he is reading this one, and then the small brief nod of satisfaction.

So I think and hope that at least my life's true work has not flown off to nonsense fantasy.

But then the accusation strikes him that I'm telling lies.

Cruelty arises from his pain; the faith in cruelty, the faith reality entirely is cruel, our universal dark belief all hope, with all its lovely perfumed vanity, is always lies. From his long familiar pain the long familiar poison antidote arises with its universal set hard grinning grimace of the jaw and its squint about the eyes and its brow pressing down.

He throws down that second card, face down too, and now grabs the box again and has them all out – 24 of them are in his hands – and, intent to tear the farce apart, he scans them fast.

Logically, there can't be anything in there to prove the dark faith that my artistic entertainment is a carnival of lies – just think carefully and plot it out; our demonstration is far past any point of that – and yet I know the hodge podge that he's thinking because I've thought it too.

First, when you first see Tarot work, you guess the cards are surely all the same, all the same and all completely vague, every one of them full of gay balloons that all fly perhaps, you guess, above vague warnings that a person must become joy and must become a friend and must become yourself and move your bowels on a proper schedule or else remain the sad unhappy wretch you are, which would, of course, answer any human question and tell any human story if you are a stupid fool.

Then perhaps you guess – after you look and see the cards are not like that at all – that this strong thing invading your brain is from The Devil, or perhaps you don't. And The Devil is real in one sense, very real: He or she or it is a lively char-acter indeed in our instinctive understanding of our lives; for when we go to war we cast our enemies or their comman-der in that role. But I don't see him doing that, or else I hope I don't.

And indeed, when the anger in him did take words it was the other anger. It was a nobler anger but not completely noble, for he has stepped into a threshold but has not stepped beyond.

First he saw the hunt for wickedness or vanity among the cards is false and gave it up. Then he dropped them on the table, laid his hands on them to keep them still. Suddenly he nailed me with a deeply bitter vivid glance, but bitter with a higher hope for decent pity rising in it.

And behind that complex glance he then declared these words out loud: "You're breaking my world!"

So I see he feels betrayed but not by me. I'm sure I understood his meaning then and understand it now, both from my own thinking now and then and from experiences before and since in years of counseling and teaching.

He felt betrayed by the incessant voices saying constantly that magic cannot happen. For indeed, he has dedicated difficult years and years to work assembling skills for human life in a prison world where a carapace of bone confines the human mind and where the human soul, if one exists at all, is pale and lifeless voiceless shadow. He has sacrificed life to that ideology and from it garnered mainly crippling pain, and now he has discovered utter proof enormous lies are in it.

Yes, he has stepped into a threshold but has not stepped on through. And so I see my Alphabeticon Tarot in this preliminary form has failed. Design Objective #3: It ought to be a soul guide teacher. I later saw The Moon in it was weak and fixed that.

He has cried, "You're breaking my world!"

In that emergency I cast my eyes into imaginary worlds to find the proper helpful answer.

I do not know it's right, that answer I then offered him, for I have never seen him since that week and scarcely shared more than mere politenesses in the few days that were left that week of our acquaintance. And it did seem harsh, somewhat, to my ears when I said it but perhaps my ears were hearing wrong and I hope I did entirely mean well for him.

I did hear it in a proper noble place when I was sitting there in human conversation after our sparse feast, casting eyes to places that I know. I heard the answer that I gave him from a darkness high and to the left, a place where – in my inborn instinct of astronomy – The Moon appears. And her answers to a wandering soul do necessarily seem harsh sometimes.

For it was this:

I waved a hand dismissingly and – in a tone that I remember as not lordly but rather scorning cowardice in a veteran senior comrade's way – I said this:

"Oh, we all get over that eventually."

So odd it seems, and yet so true.

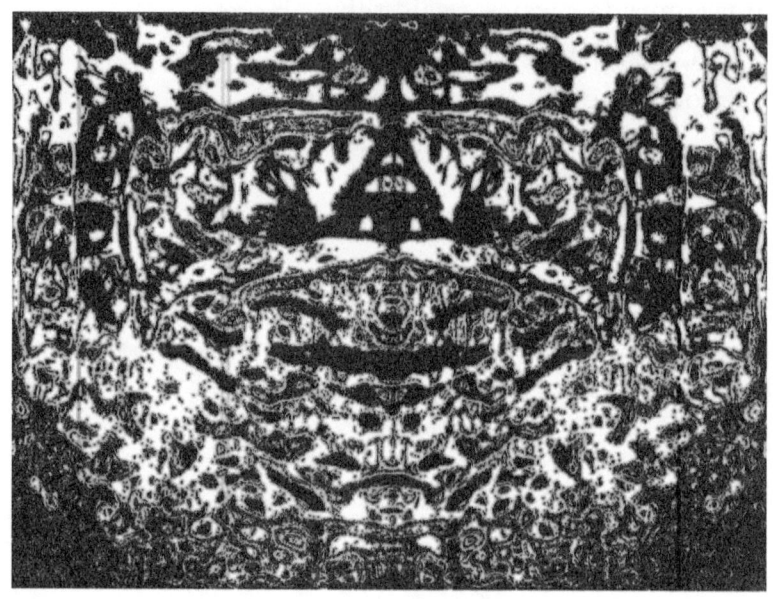

"Mysterium Tremendum"
Digital image by SR

> A Few Spiritual Technology Poems

Mysterium Tremendum

The tremendous fascinating mystery
which we can easily see
each time we look out at the world
looks back at us too,
and it beholds us
with an infinite number of eyes.

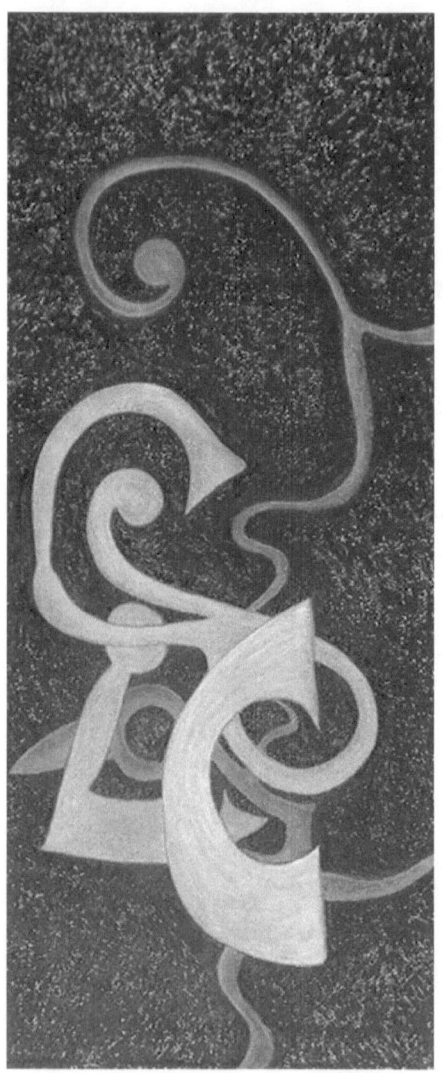

"Four Art Projects"
Painting on canvas by SR

Reawakening

'Twas moonless night. 'Twas early Spring.
'Twas in a sheltered valley pass
amid the highest uplands of the Windy Hills.
And here beneath a starry sky,
so black and cold, so deep and still,
here lay a mirror lake awaiting.
Stars above and stars below,
from depths of sky and lake they shone,
their eerie shadow bathing Earth
and filling all the distant world
with secret song.

A footloose wanderer, a nighttime walker,
the seeker of a strong and noble soul,
leaning on a staff of oaken wood,
stood drunken with the beauty
of this haunted place which welcomed him.
Perhaps he was not here.
Perhaps he lay somewhere
wrapped in his cloak beside a dying fire
and dreaming.

Bright Venus drew him on.
Above the farther hill stood silver Venus,
beacon of the dusk and dawn.
Her light shot to his heart.
She drew his footsteps down
across the grassy slope, across the pebble shore,
until he stopped with boot heels on the Earth
and toes into the water where,
gazing in the mirror depths,
he knelt to pray.

Continued ...

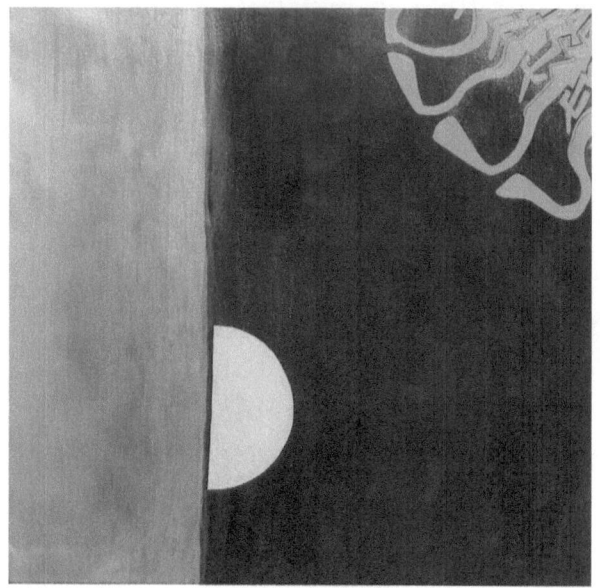

"Gazing Within"
Painting on canvas by SR

... Continued

Why do the hearts of men
reach out beyond their ken?
Why does an earthly soul forswear its bonds
to journey forth and there commune with gods?
There are no men and gods.
There is no Earth and Sky.
There is no one but One Forever Singing.

Eyes fluttered open. His own face,
all translucent in the deep and all aglow,
gazed back through dreaming eyes.
No more a mortal man, what was he now?
A shadow in the lake? A shadow in the air?
Or just a song?

This moment fear was gone.
This moment when a seeker gazed
in through him in the deep
his soul was everywhere,
so doubt was washed away.

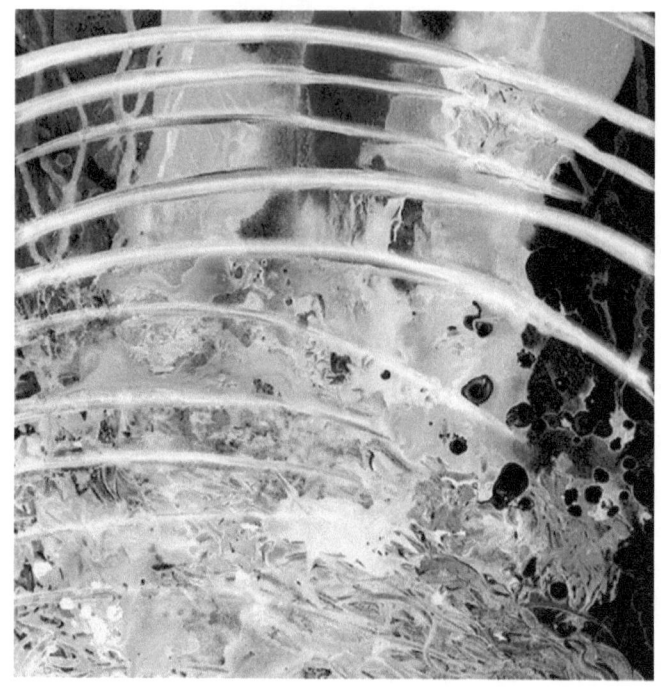

"Awaking In A Dream"
Detail of a painting on canvas by SR

Awaking In A Dream

There are many tales, of course, of Lao Tzu who, according to the legends, wrote The Watercourse Way, a little book of nature poetry upon which other thinkers then built up the lean, beautiful and tough spiritual philosophy of Taoism. Here's one of them.

The story flies us to the early morning of a day when our hero was a bright but sorrowful young man. He was a bureaucratic junior clerk in the palace of a rich and brutal warlord prince. The sparkling morning and the budding springtime garden grounds through which he trod to work belied the torment in the young man's soul. This day's duty was to be an awful deed which no one with an open heart could ever wish.

The garden path led on across a footbridge on a lovely brook and, setting foot onto the rising boards, his paces further slacked. His gaze was beckoned to the sparkling water. On the arch's highest little height the now unconscious footsteps stopped and – mind, heart and soul – he found himself drawn out into the clear deep rippling stream.

This was the moment when a human asks of "there" and "here". As another poet wrote, do I dream the butterfly or does the butterfly dream me? Gazing deep into the world I see only countless things which mirror me, so what are "you" and "I" and what am "I" to do?

But in this young man's mind no riddle of that sort found any weight. The doubtless fundamental knowledge that this clarity exists would henceforth lure and guide his thoughts and steps. The beauty of reality had ravished Lao Tzu and he was struck with lifelong love.

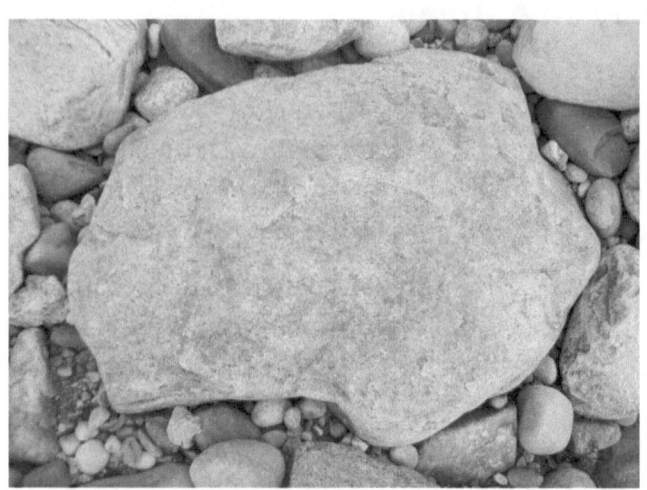

"Fine Day On Rocky Neck Beach"
Digital photo by SR

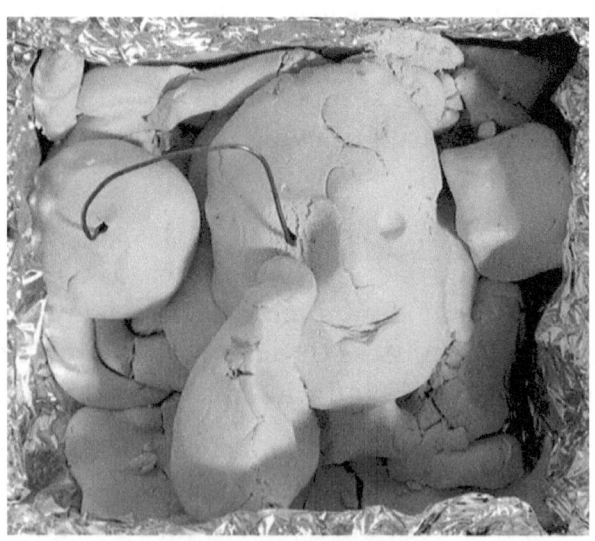

"Self Portrait With Eye Disease"
Small sculpture of polymer clay, aluminum
foil and a steel wire paper clip by SR

Always Remember

Live, love, dance
and you will never be alone.

Teaching

We human beings delight in teaching,
gifting to each other information pregnant
with its truth and usefulness and beauty.
This love is essential to our survival.

The Fig Tree
: Where The Paintings Came From

Document #5

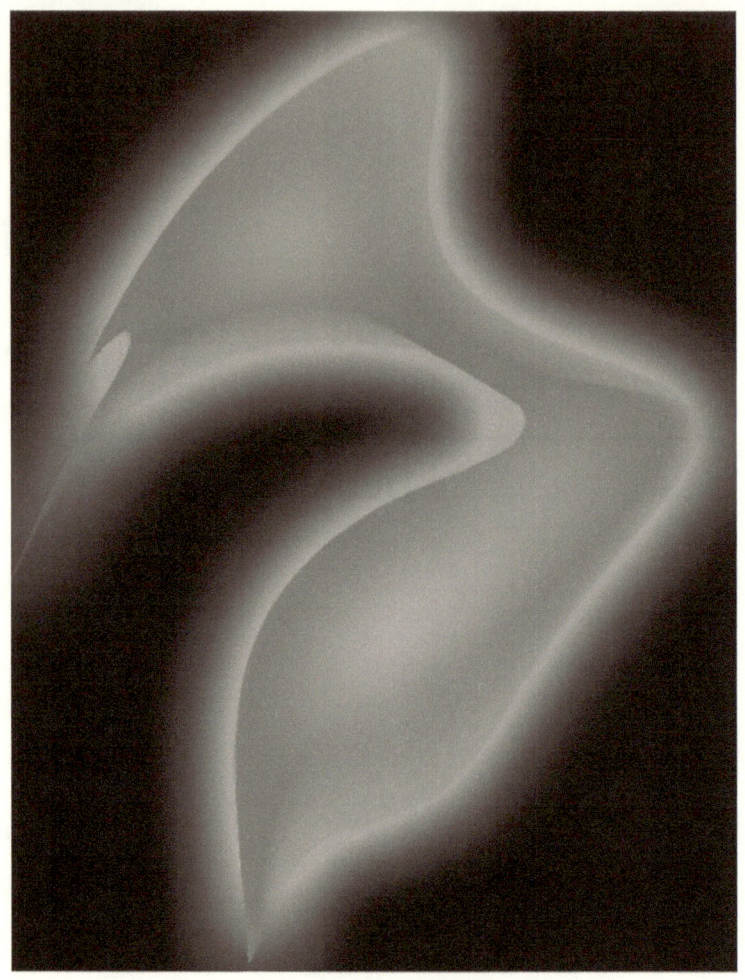

"The Fig Tree"
Digital image by SR

The Fig Tree:
Where The Paintings Came From
(Document #5)

Beauty is our surest source of Wisdom; Nature is our clearest source of Beauty; Love for each other is our strongest voice of Nature.

There was a fig tree where I was a child, filling one corner of our little house's little yard. Its beauty was amazing.

Indeed, after my childhood study of that tree, beauty seemed so mysteriously far beyond human knowing that the word "beauty" seldom even passed my lips for the next forty-odd years. Instead, I would speak and think of "joy" as the real spiritual fundamental of existence.

I would remember stretching out my little self through the summer's sweet close fragrant shade along thick viney limbs, the green light kaleidoscopic in my human eyes, the stiff big leaves rustling like paper in the breeze but so fuzzy against human skin, the fruit so strange and good. In unaccountable entwining ways the fig tree was perfection far past knowing. That was beyond.

But joy was inside me. I am joyful; I exist. That was knowable and known.

Then suddenly there was another summer day – me now far away and fifty-five years old but still there consciously a spirit in the fig tree – but now knowing more.

Now suddenly my self was felt to be obviously the viney wood – the sun soaked leaves, the strange good fruit and all – and all of this was known by its self, the self which was its self, my own self, to be extremely beautiful surpassing joy.

Of course the mode of this awakening, at last, was erotic love.

• • •

I was a lonely quiet child, for so I learned to be and learned I was. Happy laughter sprang up from my heart quite naturally, but in that house it found poor nourishment.

Our mother, from some cause forever now uncertain – perhaps her father's early death and then her brother's then her mother's – was a worried and sometimes despairing woman.

Our father, though he was the one who set the fig tree sapling in its place, was a very earnest brooding man. His childhood had been wounded by starvation poverty and then his youth by the desperate struggle of panic fear and dauntless courage in a great war.

This woman and man who made us – a girl, a boy, another boy who was myself, and then another girl – did right by us. Their love proved itself by unstinted labor that fed and housed and clothed us year after year, and in a gentle discipline that taught so well. They gave us health, honesty, literacy and cleanliness.

But love was not spoken in that house. It did not speak nor was it spoken. There was no tender touch. There were no kisses. There was not even wishing for a kiss.

• • •

In my childhood study of the backyard tree, the thing I noticed most was the viney kind of curve its trunks, branches and twigs all made. I have tried ever since, in poetry and paint, in clay between the fingertips, in word and deed, in every art, to make that powerful curve.

It was a compound line reporting all the aspects of reality at all points it inhabited, the gravity and wind and sun and mechanical adhesion in the fibers of its wood and its evolution through previous habitats and its role in the evolution of habitats and the moral tendencies of the universe and plenty more sublimely joyful dancing fluid interactions of reality far outside my knowing.

That is to say, I understood the curving of the fig tree was extremely real. It was much more real than my unconvincing notions of my self.

And so passed forty years and more, although with various awkward twists as I tried to stretch my self into that viney curve and never figured how.

• • •

That summer I was fifty-five, I was in New England.

I was renting half of a strange ramshackle house on an unworked farm. This house's other half was rented by another fellow.

You'd surely say it was a run down place but he was doing photographs and I was doing paintings and it was a joyful spot. It was a four acre hay field hilltop deep in the highlands of big woods with a mountain view that would pop your eyes out. There was delicious air.

And that was new to me. The only thing in my experience you might compare it to was oceanside air – an air also full with fragrant palpable infinities of distant large and moving things about their business – but in this fragrant air of mountain hilltop, a place full of forest beings who cast perfume on the air, this very open and very clear bright but deep green place where you would see Sky and World in every glance, and you would constantly see it all flow with storm or breeze or flow with rain or vanish into snow, there I felt myself alive among infinities.

Beside an ocean, in whatever weather, I've always felt myself in danger and a foreign traveler. But here I somehow became immediately a native of the wooded hills.

Well, the other renter there, the art photographer, was a thoughtful fellow, lonely, very nice, courteous, kind. He lent me a valuable photo reference book to make a sketch and I gifted back a tiny canvas that he fancied. I'd feed his cat when asked. Now and then we had some tea and chat.

He, my good neighbor, attended regularly at a Buddhist monastery that was there, nearby somewhere among those hills, for their silent walking contemplative retreats were a spiritual treasure to him.

Me, I had my girlfriend up on weekends quite a lot.

This lady was the very person I had absolutely given up any hope of ever finding.

In fact, I had carefully calculated the arithmetical unlikelihood that she could be alive on the same side of the planet as myself and was mistaken. I had composed a philosophic poem in which her nonexistence stood as proof of something in the universe. That is to say, logic had failed me completely in the search for her.

And I could not possibly even list the lady's charms – her forthright honesty and grace and wit and intelligence and generosity and strong insistent heart that was proven so amply since, for through her virtues she would later save my life – because at that time when we had only recently met, I mainly saw her virtues only through an utterly compelling intuition that could not be itemized.

And she was similarly bewildered by this peculiar creature me. Indeed, both our feelings seemed to be that we must simply throw away caution and absolutely work this out as we went along.

And our next door neighbor is a quiet lonely visual artist guy familiar with Oriental stuff.

And I guess you may have seen the famous photos of those old Hindu temples where sinuous entwining love-making couples, all smiling very sweetly as they serenely consummate the universe, adorn every sacred temple archway and pillar.

You may even be aware that the ornamental vegetation crafted in those famous temple carvings – the curving viney trunks and limbs and sheltering leaves which those famous undying lovers inhabit and enact so joyfully – are, of course, unmistakably fig trees. Those sculptured fig trees are, to be precise, the same ficus religiosa species under which the Buddha sat for his awakening.

And, you understand, in the past year, since months before we found each other, I had achieved sudden astonishing success in making beautiful paintings without yet knowing beauty is real. Repeat: without yet waking to the fact beauty is real.

Many paintings that will become Spirit Hill Tarot, if I may explain, were already crowded cheek by jowl among the others nailed up on my small rooms' walls – waiting since before I even knew that she exists – to greet her when she ventured up into the hills then stepped into my door, while others of them waited stacked among the leaning piles of canvases in every dusty corner.

Me painting like a lunatic, sawing and nailing frames between the painting sessions, me wondering what in the world I'm doing for all those months before she came.

• • •

So finally one day it is a lovely summer Saturday or Sunday.

A breeze that is quite irresistibly intoxicating in its meadow forest fragrance and also bursting with glowing sunlight radiance has all day been absolutely flooding the place through our open windows, all of which are open you may be sure.

She and I are cuddling, lounging very dishabille, luxuriantly satisfied for now, me more luxuriantly satisfied than I have ever been before in my entire half century life, you may be sure, and her too by every indication. Here we are in our little boudoir that opens on the universe, our little living room, which is at the back of the house where the wide window view of our steep round grassy hilltop, surrounded by the forest mountains, is more stunning.

It is a little room where big bright canvases over-filled with glowing shamanic vision and shining paint (three future Spirit Hill Tarot cards chief among them) cover all the walls above the tiny boundless island where we abide, we each touching each a fellow soul in the utmost holy intimacy of love.

I am growing actually hallucinogenic breathing in the scented light, studying the tactile structure of the mantic glowing visions that sunlight is sculpting on the breeze-blown moving sail-like surfaces of canvas stretched on wood above us.

When any human being starts to seriously explore their mind, to let it work and see what gifts it brings, they will very soon – very soon – feel the pretended boundary between their self and all the world dissolve. They may take courage in that vast mysterious state instead of fear. They may find their other self who is native there and lend that self a voice and eyes and hands and sex in this world here. So come many acts of brilliant creativity.

For me – I who have learned to trust my soul who lives there beyond, learned to marvel at its workings – to me by then there comes as well a kind of saturated dumb and sotted fullness, a savoring and keen surrender – there comes a fascinated and delicious utter giving of myself into the flowing energy of creativity as to the flowing bowl of ancient Dionysus.

So I am drunk with her and I have been forever so it seems, ever since at least our first kisses waking in that day's transcendent and transparent waking dream. And even so, the endless hour is still morning.

So Neighbor knocks. He's knocking on our front door, not the back, doesn't see us but the cars are out there out front so he figures we must be here somewhere and he shouts a loud friendly confident hello.

I realize, suddenly, Neighbor will next definitely walk around out back, searching for us in the yard, sun-bathing out there with books perhaps as we often are, and there he will quite discretely peek into our living room's wide picture window just the way that I would do undoubtedly if the situation were somehow horribly reversed, and so I bellow back an answer.

After all, the lady has another life as a Quite Respectable Person who dresses very presentably you may be sure for a professional occupation in a city and goes home to the company of three dearly loved adult daughters who, I'm absolutely sure, cast unrelenting aspersions on the old nasty Hippie freak in the woods to whom their mom is inexplicably attached and to whom, therefore, I really don't want the lady carrying home a displeasing report.

So now I'm suddenly struggling to get this emergency sorted inside my head while rummaging among the bedclothes for yesterday's trousers.

The lady is amused. She pulls a sheet up to her chin.

• • •

So here stand two men, a screen door between them.

One stands out there in the stunning brilliant summer day, a bright day, standing on the doorstep looking up, outside looking in, holding a hand up to shade his eyes.

The other is an old stout fellow naked to the waist, silver hair and beard a tangled mass around his face, blinking and squinting there in the deep shade of the hallway, inside the dark screen door which he does not open.

But the old stout guy is leaning sideways now, bending like the hilltop willow tree that stands out there beyond the cars and little gravel parking lot, slouching onto the door frame. He has expended his reserves in dragging to the door and is now overcome with a peculiar exhausted relaxation. He is trying to button his pants.

Both men know there is a woman in there.

So of course I am examining this memorable situation. Of course I'm thinking Darwin thoughts about how Nature is our lives and we are Nature.

From this new perspective of Darwin dynamics I suddenly see that all this body love is biologically powerfully recruiting me to join a Clan that sorely needs a good Grandfather because Babies are coming soon and the Matriarch of which suspects that she has stumbled on a quite exceptional candidate.

So my old lonely heart swells with relief and pride: She has chosen me for good reason. And I feel the blossoming of tender love that famous poets speak: Like a rose bloom erupting marvelously on a withered stem, I fall in love with her. That then suddenly disproves all my theorems of grief, so suddenly I begin at once surrendering the doubt and fear which all that loneliness always gave me.

But Neighbor is talking, as he has a right, shrugging ruefully, reminding me, apologetic since he clearly feels ridiculous – and maybe even feels made a fool and maybe even hurt – about the very interesting old wrecked beaver dam in the woods a pleasant walk away from there which he did mention a couple weeks ago one time, to his suggestion which I did indeed answer him that the lady and I would probably like to walk out for a look and to which he is going now to make some photos that are going to be very fine in this very fine light, so he shrugs again. And would we like to go?

And here, for your information, let me just interject that I am still sorry and embarrassed – ashamed somewhat in fact – that I never went with my good Neighbor to see that beaver dam which would have been interesting.

But now, in my intoxicated state, I am carried off by thoughts about the tender poignancy of life. I used to be so much like Neighbor just so recently and for so long before. And he is me of course. I have escaped that fate but should I rejoice or mourn? Of course I must do both and in them both know joy.

In fact, I am at last surrendering what remains of the fear and doubt my loneliness for so long gave me.

• • •

So now I hear a footstep in the hall and turn and look.

Now comes the Lady in her person.

I have heard her step and looked and seen her coming from the living room into the hall.

And she is there.

I gape.

She is appropriately clothed. She wears her lover's shirt from yesterday, Gypsy bangles at her ears and silver finger rings. The shirt falls just exactly long enough to cast the Sacred Mysteries of Venus respectfully in shadow. In the hallway's dark this gleaming female soul is glorious.

I either gasp or moan.

So the Lady is in the doorway by me now, within the darkly veiling screen. So the entryway is filled; no one will enter. She takes my arm in hers and strikes a friendly pose and says hello to Neighbor.

Neighbor's eyes fly to a spot in the air above and there they stay. But he says hello. Furthermore, he briefly, with quite commendable aplomb, outlines the friendly invitation to a scenic woodland ramble.

Before she speaks to answer him, she moves. It may be at first a gesture simply answering the friendly invitation in some normal way but then it is a dance. It becomes unmistakably an artist's pose.

Then it is indeed an apt quotation from great famous art which Neighbor loves, great art I know he loves because this pose of hers is photographed exactly and repeatedly in a photo reference book of South Asian temple architecture he recently took from his private shelf and opened to those pages of those photos with a lover's tender touch and then generously lent that book to me his painter neighbor.

In this brief dance, this divine erotic dance, the Lady took my arm to wrap around her back to put my hand exactly at her waist and there she holds it, her hand pressing mine with every silent signal of human touch that I must hold that curve of her fervent soul in strength.

So we are relaxed and yet we have embraced securely. And so, if I may say it in this way, the Lady's substance entwines in mine:

Her other hand goes up behind us, appearing on my farther shoulder and it grips; she gives her weight. She lifts her far foot just enough to put its heel above her near foot's ankle, so her knee arising slightly as the toe points obliquely down. So she is reclining on me like I am reclining in such languor on the wooden doorway post and I feel her relax, her substance now becoming mine so familiarly in an act of love.

So what is this? Are we truly beings carved above the temple threshold steps, truly? Are we not? For this blessed place where all this glorious mysterious art is done for such hidden reasons; is this not a place of miracles for that whole summer long – which has not ended yet – and are we not its clergy?

Somehow in true, true fact – in facts somehow assembled there out of the actual substance of reality by brilliant workings done in beauty – we are the fig tree now. And thus the powerful reality of beauty has been proved.

For me this is an ecstasy. And it resolves deep riddles of human joy and meaning.

I Guess We Will Arise

: Prospects For The Future

Document #6

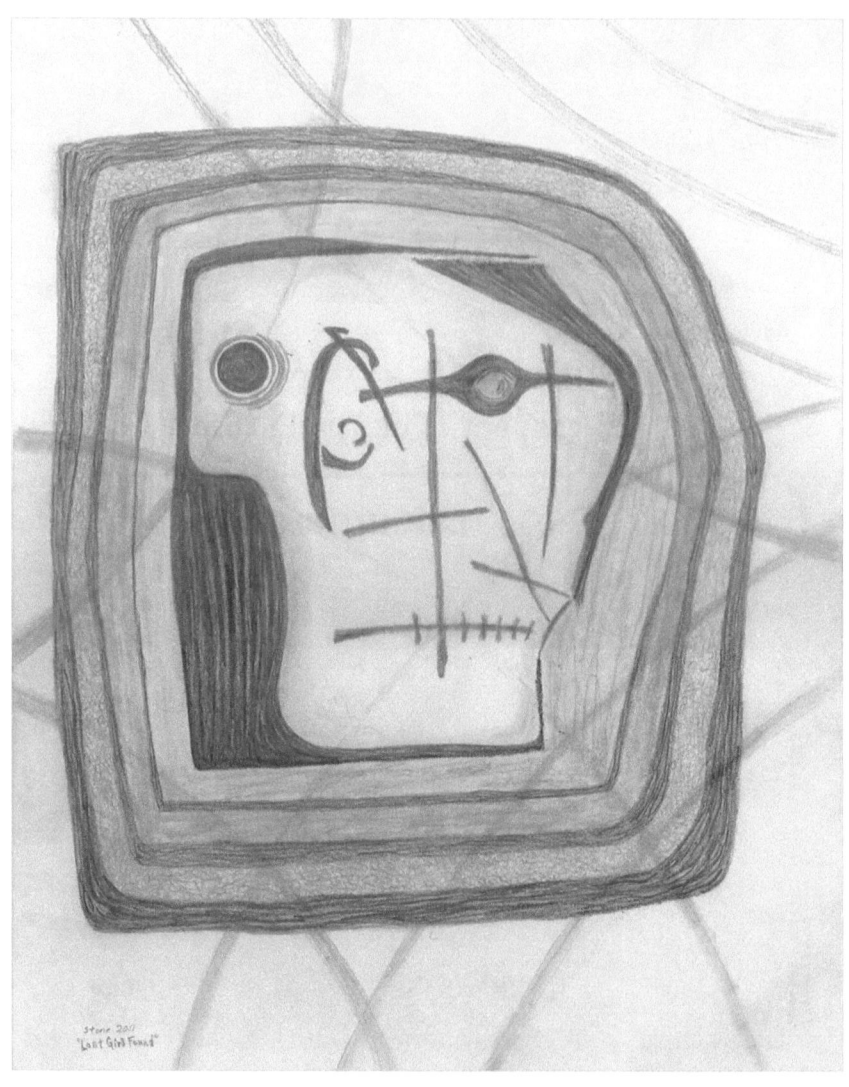

"Lost Girl Found"
Drawing by Stone Riley
Graphite pencil on bristol paper.
A wandering youth who discovered
friends and work in the Occupy camp.

I Guess We Will Arise:
Prospects For The Future
(Document #6)

Lost Girl Found

Oh dear and darling daughter
whom I knew for brief and passing days,
you of grief and will to worthy deeds
here in this world,
and human failings too;

I pray all goddesses who ever are
in past and future present time,
to fill your life with worthy deeds
and blessedness and peace
and hero's glory.

> To Make A World

I guess we will arise in our democracy very soon.
Shaking off our long hypnotic sleepy spell of doubt we'll
sweep away like dust all these preposterous tyrannies of
greed and slaughter that pretend to rule us now. Just look
around yourself and see: The great rebellion's waking
moment is already here.

For the criminal demands on us have grown far too
ridiculous to bear in our accustomed fearful meek confused
obedience, and our meekness was the only strength the so-
called rulers had.

We only must refuse to obey them in steadfast unity –
and we must love each other – and the tyrants will fall.

So look around to look for that moment coming and suddenly – this year, this month, this week, today – you'll see every kind of human being now marching in the streets together.

So now while we refine and prove our unity in strength – proving our truth enforcing force straight through every fear and pain – now more and more of our human kin are rushing to the struggle. If love and courage do grow and continue in our hearts, victory is now assured.

Yes, we and ours will suffer in this rising – for our opponents are insane and, as the whole world knows, they torture just as freely as they kill – so this then too: the voluntary discipline we must adopt of practical and spiritual non-violence is hard – but aren't we and ours and all the world already suffering harder than that now?

So then, when we have chosen freedom decisively and irreversibly – when we have in great majority chosen to seek reality as recognized by our own eyes and our own souls – when we have grown deaf to the tyrants' endless pitiless preposterous crippling lies denying what we are – then our freedom will inevitably be real.

Then, finally when we have won that fight – when we have won that struggle to decide the shape and contour of the New Age at its birth – then certainly we will discover utter depths of grief that human souls have never known before, for we will then be free to mourn all that were murdered in the age when murder ruled supreme.

And in that holy sacrificial state of grief we can begin to heal the Goddess Earth.

But can a new age be different from the old? That is to say, can we be different human beings than before when we were deathly sick with loneliness? We can and will.

"Tintern Abbey" is a nature poem by William Wordsworth composed in Wales in 1798. It's often said to be his best loved work.

In the sweet touching rhythm of its verse the poet tells that he is visiting a very beautiful valley he last visited in youth. Now he is grown older. Now the hardness of the human world has changed him, quenched a sort of desperate delirium for beauty he felt then.

And now here this scene he sees is real. This is a real valley, not the land of sweet fair dreamy memory that kept his faith in gentle human life alive through coarser years.

And yet the poet reassures us finally – convinces us – that it is good and that it feeds the soul.

By the poem's end we are willing to hear and feel that reassurance because along the way he has proved extraordinary familiarity with spiritual affairs, by vividly describing some of our most profound sensations of the movements of our souls in quite realistic detail.

So we should listen to this Wordsworth person on our current pressing emergency question of what nourishment a normal healthy human soul requires. Will such food be available to our human race in coming times?

Well, in this poem Wordsworth tells us this:

First he recognizes now that human beings take part in the natural world and he now welcomes that duty and he says we can do it well.

Next he tells a joyful spiritual experience of our human presence in the soul of Nature, for he now sees that we are soul-deep in the mountains and the meadows and the vast blue sky and all.

But finally he rejoices that his beloved human mate is there, his soul mate sister – to reflect, share and then remember – so these internal things are real. And in their companionship, when they are together, that's when the poet sings the highest praises of the nourishment that Nature brings his soul.

That is to say, Nature sets a spiritual feast before us when our human company arrives together.

And that, I think, is brilliant wisdom.

And I'm starting to see a working program in it: How about you and I each find some beautiful small poetic quote, some very small but brilliant line, which tells the actual fact that "I am you and we are All entire." (That one is from William Blake.)

Now memorize the little bit you picked. Probably think up some slightly fuller way to say it too, 20 words or less, for when you're asked.

(If you prefer a currently living author and don't know where to look, my first suggestion would be "The Faraway Nearby" which is a recent book by Rebecca Solnit.)

Now every time you're in a meeting where people are pretending that vitally important fact is not true – this would be a political, religious, government or business meeting maybe, or a book club or a barroom chat – where people are pretending like human beings, or some human beings, are separate and apart, or pretending like we're not all part of Earth – then let's you and me just stand up and just say our little bit as a reminder that actually "I am you and we are All entire".

Since most anyone who just consciously thinks about it for a moment discovers they already know it's true and it is good and sacred, and since more and more people today are waking up from a hypnotic trance and starting to think consciously, then this action plan, or something like it, might have good results.

It would be like inviting people to a feast.

Maybe even, come to think about it, as our culture changes, that very beautiful vision of sacred unified reality might eventually become instituted in our changing culture as some kind of on-going permanent communal planetary celebration feast of Nature's spiritual gifts.

And I guess that would be a key to the Good Reality of the New Age for all of Earth and for our human race.

> And My Proposal To You

My main project in Tarot – and in all my lifetime work – has been to show that we can do brilliant things.

We human beings do brilliant deeds, great deeds, when such deeds are needed and when certain virtues – joy in truth, willful courage, consciousness of freedom, love for all that lives – are awake in us. We have enormous powers waiting at our fingertips, only waiting for us to remember how to summon them.

This is true: Despite our universal suffering and fear and shame – despite our many weaknesses – in these days we will do brilliant deeds because we can and must awake our virtues.

And in this piece of my lifetime work I have a special purpose for revealing your secret powers: With this book, which is primarily a tale of virtues, I am trying to recruit you as a teacher and a healer.

So if I may,
I recommend to you the blessings of The Sun and Moon.

About The Author

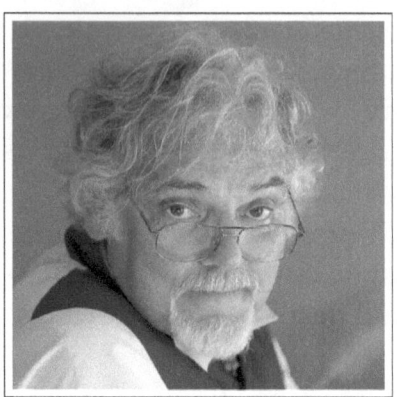

Stone Riley
Photo by Evelina Kremsdorf
Used by permission.

Who Is Stone Riley?
April 2015:
I'm an old artist / activist / fortune teller.
Been doing all of that for 50 years.

    I practice arts – painting, drawing, computer, poetry, memoir, the novel, teaching, conversation, conversation – some of it quite well. After all, I work hard at it, love a challenge, love doing it myself, first hand, in person. Because, of course, the most beautiful of all beautiful art is supposed to be your life and I love life. You study, study, study, practice, practice practice – of course you do – but this is a dance.

    I came up as a working stiff so-called-white boy in a dirty dangerous industrial city in neo-slavery land, the jim crow USA South, came up just in time for the Vietnam War machine to murder a friend of mine in our youth. All that made of me a lifelong pro-peace pro-Earth pro-human pro-democracy agitating activist more or less, at least jumping up into that kind of work when opportunity presents. I am now a Green Party member and I'm optimistic now at last because it seems the tide has turned.

And fortune telling? What? Why that? Well, if life has ever put you in a circumstance to sit with some weeping woman and help her share a last farewell with a loved one lost beyond the veil - and you've judged the ghost there in the room definitely is somehow real although apparently only you can see it clear enough - if fate has vouchsafed you that piece of work just once, that joy and kindly tender pleasure most sublime, then you won't ask me why I also do that sort of job.

And really it's all one.

The great art philosopher Rabindranath Tagore certainly described how I started out. Tagore described the proper way to start an art career like this: First you look around where you are and see what is most horrible there. Then from that you see what is most beautiful. Then, being who you are, you ask how art work there can aid the beautiful. And so you have begun.

When I started work our nation was a prison nation, our every thought a prisoner's thought. So we did enormous crimes. That was the horror. So the greatest loveliness I saw was freedom of the mind, and the broadest cleanest most cour-ageous freedom our young generation did was this: Rebirth the perennial undying spiritual technologies which are common property of human kind and know we are divine. What was there for me to do in that?

I wished to make myself a proper artist. There were some pictures people raved about, very hard profound pictures somehow stacked up neatly in a deck. And then an initial one-year project in Tarot vastly exceeded all my hopes. Tarot proved itself at once to be the most profound of politics: an instrument of mercy shared among us prisoners. And then I grew into it. It became my guide book in the art of democratic life, for it made a healing teaching priest of me.

So here's my advice:

Don't stop walking when there is no way ahead.
    Your walking makes the path.
    The place you started from was cleared by others
        and others will soon follow you
        and pass and step ahead.

Philosophic Note

The thinking in this book is profoundly influenced
by the Seth Material and deeply indebted to the work
of Jane Roberts and Robert Butts.

Internet Links

Stone Riley's main website: www.stoneriley.com

His website about Tarot: www.stoneriley.com/tarot

www.ingramcontent.com/pod-product-compliance
Lightning Source LLC
Chambersburg PA
CBHW030810180526
45163CB00003B/1217